The Fort Burgwin Research Center

A partial list of publications written, edited, or compiled by Fred Wendorf

A Report on the Excavation of a Small Ruin near Point of Pines, East Central Arizona (1950)

Archaeological Studies in the Petrified Forest National Monument (1953)

The Midland Discovery: A Report on the Pleistocene Human Remains from Midland, Texas (1955)
With A. D. Krieger, C. C. Albritton, and T. D. Stewart

Paleoecology of the Llano Estacado (1961)

Contributions to the Prehistory of Nubia (1965)

The Prehistory of Nubia (1968)

A Middle Stone Age Sequence from the Central Rift Valley of Ethiopia (1974)
With R. Schild and C. C. Albritton

The Prehistory of the Nile Valley (1976)
With R. Schild

Prehistory of the Eastern Sahara (1980)
With R. Schild

The Prehistory of Wadi Kubbaniya, 3 vols. (1989)
With R. Schild and A. E. Close, assemblers and editors

Egypt During the Last Interglacial: The Middle Paleolithic of Bir Tarfawi and Bir Sahara East (1993)
With R. Schild and others

Holocene Settlement of the Egyptian Sahara, Volume 1: The Archaeology of Nabta Playa (2001)
With R. Schild and Associates

The Fort Burgwin Research Center

FRED WENDORF

With James E. Brooks

Published in cooperation with the
William P. Clements Center for Southwestern Studies

SOUTHERN METHODIST UNIVERSITY
Dallas

First edition, 2007

Cover image by W.W. Anderson. Courtesy of Mrs. Virginia S. White and family.
Cover and text design by Tom Dawson

Library of Congress Cataloging-in-Publication Data

Wendorf, Fred.
The Fort Burgwin Research Center / Fred Wendorf with James E. Brooks. —1st ed.
p. cm.
ISBN 978-0-9795372-0-2 (alk. paper)
1. Fort Burgwin Research Center—History. I. Brooks, James E. II. Title.

LD5101.S36565F678 2007
370.72—dc22

2007014400

Printed in the United States of America on acid-free paper

10 9 8 7 6 5 4 3 2 1

Contents

Preface

BEGINNING MORE THAN FIFTY YEARS AGO, IN THE SUMMER OF 1956, AND continuing today, a beautiful small mountain valley located ten miles south of Taos, New Mexico, was the scene of an important experiment in the development of a center for research and teaching in the sciences, the humanities, and the arts. With a half-dozen others, I was privileged to have a central part in this experiment, the details of which are not well-known to the public. Because most of the other principal players in this effort are no longer alive to recount the history, I decided to tell the story, or at least my part in it, before it is lost forever.

Located within this mountainous area of the Little Rio Grande Valley was a pre–Civil War U.S. Army post known as Cantonment Burgwin (1852–60). The archaeological excavation and restoration of this army post provided the initial stimulus for the development of what eventually came to be known as SMU-in-Taos. This western campus of Southern Methodist University (SMU) began as the Fort Burgwin Research Center, an independent research facility focused on the field sciences, the humanities, and the arts and supported by the Rounds Foundation of Wichita, Kansas, supplemented by occasional grants from the National Science Foundation for specific research projects. The Center was conceived by Ralph M. Rounds, a prosperous lumberman from Wichita, who envisioned the Research Center as a means of contributing to the scholarly and intellectual growth of northern New Mexico.

Rounds owned several large timber areas in the western part of the United States, but his favorite property was the Rancho del Rio Grande Grant, consisting of approximately 91,000 acres of piñon, ponderosa, fir, aspen, and spruce forest located south and east of Taos. With George Lavender, a Santa Fe, New Mexico, lumberman who also had interests in archaeology and history, Rounds operated a large sawmill on the Rancho del Rio Grande Grant near the confluence of two creeks, the Little Rio Grande and the Rito de la Olla (Pot Creek). Rounds had a keen interest in history, and he knew from the title abstract to the grant that an army post had once stood somewhere on his property, but its exact location was not known. He had tried to find the post, and in the early 1950s he had brought in two historians to help in the search, but all attempts had been unsuccessful.

The following is a history of Fort Burgwin Research Center and how it eventually became SMU-in-Taos. It is an interesting story, cut short by the untimely death of the initial sponsor, Ralph Rounds. Had Rounds lived a few years longer, there might have been a very different outcome, although not necessarily a better one.

Today, the 300-plus-acre campus of Fort Burgwin belongs to SMU and functions as the western campus of the university. Every year between May and October, some two hundred students and faculty from the main university campus in Dallas come to the Sangre de Cristo Mountains of north-central New Mexico to participate in a learning experience that is unique among U.S. universities. Taos, with its blend of Pueblo Indian, Spanish, and Anglo cultures, provides one important dimension of this experience. A second and equally important asset is the campus itself. Nestled in a beautiful mountain valley and surrounded by the Carson National Forest, the campus is an ideal setting for learning and scholarship, particularly in the field sciences and the creative arts. The nearby countryside also offers a wealth of places of natural and historic interest.

It was my good fortune to have been involved with the Fort Burgwin Research Center from the very beginning. I served as the director for the first twenty years and as an interested onlooker after 1976. I feel great pleasure that so many of the goals of the initial benefactor have been achieved since the Center became a part of SMU, my academic home beginning in 1964. This is a personal document, with most of the data drawn from copies of the reports I submitted to the board that was established to govern the Research Center. I think this is a reasonably accurate statement of what happened and, in a few instances, of why events unfolded as they did.

When James E. Brooks became Associate Provost and Dean of Faculties of Humanities and Sciences in 1969, he assumed administrative responsibility for the Fort Burgwin Research Center from Dean Claude Albritton. Brooks retained that responsibility until 1984, when the Center became fully integrated into SMU. After I resigned as Director of Fort Burgwin in 1976, Jim—by then Provost of the university—became even more involved in the operation of the Research Center. He also developed closer ties with the Taos community. He had a pivotal role in keeping the Research Center functioning. Without his support and guidance, the development of Fort Burgwin and the interest of SMU in the Center might have been different. To complete the story about Fort Burgwin, and to gain his insight, I invited Brooks to write about the activities during this period and how he coped with the complications that arose. His story is presented here as Chapter 4.

Acknowledgments

One of the most difficult aspects of assembling a history book is finding photographs of those who were important to the story, particularly when almost all of the major players are dead. Moreover, such a book needs illustrations to help the reader visualize what happened and what the participants looked like. I never imagined that this story would be written, and so I gave little thought to creating a photographic record. I did not begin assembling photographs of those now gone until after I sent an early copy of my text to Thomas W. Tunks, Associate Provost at Southern Methodist University. After reading the text, Tunks urged me to find the photographs, polish the text, and prepare the manuscript for publication. He realized that few people knew the complete story of how Fort Burgwin, now the western campus of the university and known as SMU-in-Taos, became a part of the university. When the text and the illustrations were ready, Tunks provided the financial resources to publish *The Fort Burgwin Research Center*. Without Tunks, the project would have languished. I am also indebted to Michael Adler, Executive Director of SMU-in-Taos, for supporting this effort and speeding it along.

Many people assisted me in improving the manuscript. I am greatly indebted to Jim Brooks for calling my attention to several chronological errors in the first draft of the text, and to Ronald K. Wetherington, my successor as Director of Fort Burgwin, for his editorial suggestions. I am also grateful to my wife, Anna Christine Bednar, and Teddy Diggs, of Diggs Publication Services, for their careful editing. All of them found mistakes that, if uncorrected, would have been embarrassing to me.

A major problem I faced was finding photographs of Ralph Rounds, the founder of Fort Burgwin, and of his two sons, Bill Rounds and Dwight Rounds. Those who helped me find photos include the widows of Bill and Dwight and their sons and daughters. Among them are Carolyn Vickers, Robert Rounds, Ed Rounds, D. C. Rounds, and Doug and Becky Neumann. Only Carolyn had known me when I was the director of Fort Burgwin, and I had lost contact with her after Bill and Dwight died. Sarah Bond, of Wichita Collegiate School, put me back in touch with Carolyn and also sent me a fine photograph of Ralph Rounds, the original of which hangs in the school. In addition, Carolyn pushed the right button, and soon I was receiving e-mails and photographs.

Several people—including Barbara Brenner, C. B. Trujillo, Jim Taylor, Palemon Cardenas, Jack Meyers, and Tony Meyers—provided photographs of Taos citizens who were part of the Fort Burgwin story. Laurie Evans Frantz, a friend and colleague now with the New Mexico Department of Tourism, helped me contact the Museum of New Mexico Photo Archive. She also introduced me to Sibel Melik, Archivist at the New Mexico Commission of Public Records. Both archives provided photographs. Additional crucial help with photographs came from Hillsman Stuart Jackson, staff photographer for SMU. An impressive technician, he scanned and edited all the photographs and drawings and sent them to SMU Press.

I also want to acknowledge the extraordinary assistance I received at the onset of the Fort Burgwin project from the late Virginia S. White, of Sumter, South Carolina, who was the daughter of W. W. Anderson, the post surgeon at Cantonment Burgwin from 1855 to 1857. She and her heirs sent me three drawings of the post by Anderson; two of the drawings are reproduced in the book.

Keith Gregory, Director, and George Ann Ratchford, Marketing and Production Manager, of Southern Methodist University Press provided design and editing assistance. I am very grateful to SMU and to SMU Press for this opportunity to tell the story of the Fort Burgwin Research Center.

CHAPTER 1

Finding, Excavating, and Rebuilding Cantonment Burgwin

In the summer of 1956, I began my association with the Fort Burgwin Research Center, eventually known as SMU-in-Taos. When the story began, I was thirty-two years old and had received my Ph.D. three years before. I already had considerable archaeological excavation experience in Arizona and New Mexico, having conducted my dissertation research in the Petrified Forest in Arizona and having directed a pipeline archaeological salvage project that extended from New Mexico to California. In 1956 I had a research job as an assistant curator at the Museum of New Mexico in Santa Fe, where, in cooperation with the New Mexico Highway Department and the Federal Bureau of Public Roads, I had developed a statewide program to salvage archaeological sites threatened by highway construction—the first such program in the United States. During the course of this activity I had met and become friends with George Lavender, then Chairman of the New Mexico State Highway Commission (Figure 1).

In the late spring of 1956, Lavender and I were attending a regional meeting of highway construction executives in Phoenix, Arizona, where I gave a lecture urging the chief highway engineers of other states to develop archaeology-salvage programs similar to the one we had developed in New Mexico. Earlier that year I had decided to leave the Museum of New Mexico, and I had just accepted a position as Associate Professor of Anthropology and Associate Director of the Museum at Texas Technological University in Lubbock.

One evening near the end of the conference, Lavender and I happened to sit next to each other at a large and rather raucous party for the New Mexico delegation. At some point during that evening, Lavender commented that he

Figure 1.
Betty and George Lavender, ca. 1970.

Photographer unknown. Photo courtesy of Barbara Brenner, Taos, New Mexico.

had heard about my planned departure for Texas and suggested that I continue my archaeological research in New Mexico. I agreed enthusiastically, and he offered to help, saying, "When we sober up, come see me."

A week or so later I called on Lavender and discovered that he not only remembered our conversation but also was familiar with a large ruin south of Taos, on land where he operated a sawmill. He suggested that this ruin, known as Pot Creek Pueblo, would be an excellent place to have an archaeological field school, and he offered to assist the field school financially. He also mentioned, however, that it was his business partner, Ralph M. Rounds (Figure 2), who owned the Rancho del Rio Grande Grant, the land where the site was located. Lavender added that Rounds had a lot more money than he and was also interested in archaeology. Lavender offered to introduce me to Rounds, who kept an apartment above the sawmill office at Pot Creek, where he often spent several weeks each summer. Lavender told me that although Rounds was likely to help me with my plans to excavate the pueblo, he was primarily interested in a pre–Civil War U.S. Army post that was thought to be located on the property. Lavender suggested that before I talked with Rounds, I should see if I could find any information about an old fort that may have been established in the area south of Taos.

Although I was not enthusiastic about spending several months looking for the remains of a fort in the mountainous area south of Taos, I decided to give the search my best effort. I spent the next few weeks conducting research, reading, among other works, *Forts and Forays: A Dragoon in New Mexico, 1850–1856,* the diary of James A. Bennett, who was a supply sergeant in the First Dragoons and who in 1852 had helped build a post near Taos known as Cantonment Burgwin. The term *cantonment* was then used by the U.S. Army to designate a temporary

Figure 2.
Ralph M. Rounds.

Photograph by Rorabaugh-Millsap Studio, Wichita, Kansas. Copy by Irelock Imaging, Medford, Oregon. Photo courtesy of Becky and Cally Vickers of Medford, Oregon, and Sarah Bond of Wichita, Kansas.

post, much as *camp* is used by the army today. I also read Lydia Spencer Lane's *I Married a Soldier; or, Old Days in the Old Army*. She had married 1st Lt. William B. Lane of the U.S. Mounted Rifles on May 18, 1854, and they were soon sent to New Mexico Territory, where they spent October and November of 1854 at Cantonment Burgwin. In her diary, Lane described the cantonment as a "very small post, most beautifully situated, being surrounded by high mountains . . . nine miles from Taos, New Mexico."

This research was helpful, but the most important information I found came from an unpublished document, a copy of which was in the Museum of New Mexico library. The original, which was in the National Archives, carried the lengthy title *Report of Jos. K. F. Mansfield, Colonel and Inspector General, United States Army, Regarding His Inspection of the Department of New Mexico during the Summer and Fall of the Year 1853*. This report gave a brief description of Cantonment Burgwin and included a map showing the cantonment's location at the confluence of the Little Rio Grande and an unnamed eastern tributary. The Mansfield map also identified and marked the location of all the buildings at the cantonment as they had existed in 1853 (Figure 3).

A quick study of the topographic sheet for the Taos area indicated that there were only two significant streams entering the Little Rio Grande from the east and that only one of them matched Lane's description as "beautifully situated, being surrounded by high mountains . . . nine miles from Taos, New Mexico." The matching stream was Pot Creek, where the Rounds and Lavender sawmill was located. During the course of my reading, I also learned that Cantonment Burgwin had been named after Captain John H. K. Burgwin, who had been killed in 1847 in an assault on the church at Taos Pueblo during the Taos Rebellion, and that the cantonment had been established on August 14, 1852, and abandoned on May 18, 1860.

Figure 3.

Map made in 1853 by Colonel Jos. K. F. Mansfield.

Photocopy by Fred Wendorf of map in the Museum of New Mexico Laboratory of Anthropology Library.

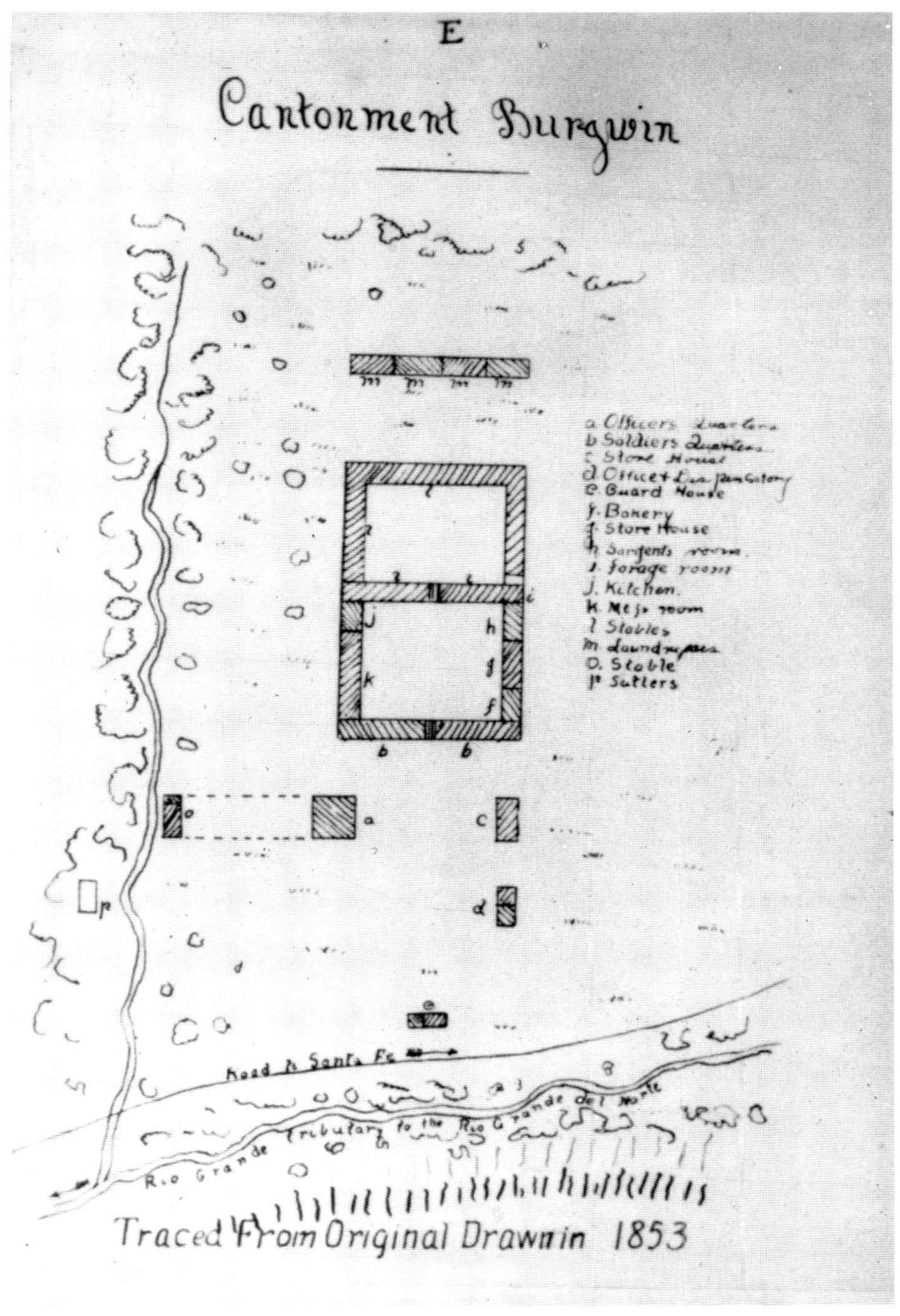
E
Cantonment Burgwin
a Officers Quarters
b Soldiers Quarters
c Store House
e Guard House
f. Bakery
g. Store House
h Sargents room
i. forage room
J. Kitchen.
k. Mess room
l Stables
O. Stable
p Sutlers
Road to Santa Fe
Rio Grande del Norte
Tributary to the Rio Grande
Rio Grande
Traced From Original Drawn in 1853

In July 1956, shortly after reviewing the Mansfield report, I received word that Rounds was in Taos and would like to meet with me, so I took the Mansfield manuscript and drove up to Taos and out to the sawmill at Pot Creek Lumber Company. The office building was located on the south side of Pot Creek, about a hundred yards east of the highway to Las Vegas. South of the office was a huge sawmill, covering about twenty-five acres, with a millpond, vast piles of logs, and stacks of sawed lumber; the whole area was bustling with people, loaders, and logging trucks.

When I got out of the car, I saw Rounds standing on his porch above the sawmill office. He waved to me and told me to come on up. Sixty-five years old and about five feet eight inches tall, Rounds was not a large man; he was solid but not fat. He had a round, friendly face and a light complexion. He was mostly bald, with tufts of sandy-gray hair above both ears.

He invited me to sit in one of the chairs at a small table, and he sat in the other chair. He immediately put me at ease by telling me that he knew I wanted to bring a group of students from Texas Tech to excavate the old pueblo located across the creek about five hundred yards north of the office. He liked the idea and said he would help financially with the project. Lavender had obviously briefed him well.

With only a moment's pause, he went on to say that even though he liked my plan to study the old pueblo, he really was interested in finding and possibly restoring the old fort that was perhaps located somewhere on his property. I told him that I was also interested in the old fort and that I had found a map (from the Mansfield report) that might help us find it. We then looked at the map, and he agreed that the cantonment seemed to have been located where Pot Creek joined the Little Rio Grande, which was about a mile north and west of the office. We immediately got into his car and drove across the highway and down a small track that bordered Pot Creek on the south and west bank. A hundred yards or so after crossing the highway (about two hundred yards from his apartment), I noticed a group of low mounds in the sagebrush flat just south of the track. I told Rounds they looked like the ruins of several small pueblos.

We followed Pot Creek to the confluence with the Little Rio Grande and got out of the car to inspect the site. It was a marshy area, not at all a promising setting for a military post. We searched anyway for about an hour but did not find a trace of anything that might be a fort. Very disappointed, we returned to the car and started back to his office. On the way back we decided to stop at the low mounds we had seen on the way down. We got out of the car and had walked about fifty feet when I found a uniform button of the First Dragoons. We also discovered horseshoes, a few .50-caliber bullets, some handmade nails, and lots of old broken glass and china, but no Indian pottery. I told Rounds that we had found Cantonment Burgwin, or at least some part of it, and that the numerous small mounds we could see in the sagebrush were likely collapsed chimneys, indicating the probable presence of several buildings. Years later I learned that Pot Creek had changed its course after the visit by Colonel Mansfield and that in 1853 it had indeed joined the Little Rio Grande as shown on the Mansfield map.

We returned to Rounds's apartment in high spirits. He recounted his previous unsuccessful efforts to find the fort and mentioned that one scholar had told him that the post was located where the sawmill now stood. Rounds asked me if I would be willing to excavate the cantonment the following summer. He said that the work at the cantonment would be in addition to excavating a part of the old pueblo.

I agreed to his proposal but noted that I was disturbed by the scholar's statement that the post was located under the sawmill. I cautioned Rounds that the sawmill might have destroyed a major part of the cantonment and that only a careful archaeological study would resolve this question. I also suggested that one of my first steps should be a search of the military records relating to Cantonment Burgwin in the National Archives, to find out as much as I could about the post and its history. He asked me to prepare a plan and a budget for the work as soon as I could after establishing myself in Lubbock.

It was at this time, I believe, that Rounds first outlined to me his long-term goal for the old fort and the Rancho del Rio Grande Grant. He told me that he had made a lot of money from the timber on the grant and that he loved New Mexico and its people. He said he wanted to use some of his money to help the region. This interest on his part led us to discuss using the reconstruction of the cantonment to create a facility where scientists, scholars, and artists could work and thereby enrich the culture and economy of the region.

Dealing with the National Archives

While still in Santa Fe, I wrote to the National Archives, outlined our project, and asked for assistance. The response was a form letter indicating that I would be welcome to use the archives but that the search would be up to me and that I could not expect to receive any help from the staff. As an archaeologist who had no experience with either old military documents or the National Archives, I knew that if I undertook the job alone, it would be very time-consuming and probably not very productive.

A few weeks later, probably in early September, and with the help of Seymour Connor, a colleague in the History Department at Texas Tech, I was able to contact a member of Senator Lyndon Johnson's staff and ask for help. Johnson was then Senate Majority Leader and one of the most influential men in Washington, D.C. The next day I learned that the senator had agreed to help me; in exchange, he asked me to pose for a photograph with him and help prepare a press release about his assistance with our project. I quickly agreed, made an appointment with the senator, and scheduled a trip to Washington for two weeks later.

When I arrived at Senator Johnson's office, another man was already waiting. I soon learned that this man was the director of the National Archives. A few minutes later a photographer appeared, the senator emerged and said hello, and the photograph was taken of Senator Johnson, the director of the National Archives, and me. With a nod to me, the senator then said, "I believe everything is taken care of," and left. The director then asked me to go with him to the National Archives. En route, I expressed my acute embarrassment over the trouble I had caused him. He replied, "Think nothing of it; when the senate majority leader asks me to do something, I do it." This whole episode would not be significant except that when we arrived at the National Archives, I discovered that the staff had laid out for me everything they could find about Cantonment Burgwin. After a brief inspection, I arranged for all of the material to be copied on microfilm for later study.

There was another, completely unexpected benefit from the assistance I received from Senator Johnson. The senator's news release about our plans to study Cantonment Burgwin was sent out nationwide, and this led to my receiving a letter from Virginia S. White, of Sumter, South Carolina. White was the daughter of W. W. Anderson, who had been stationed at Cantonment Burgwin as Post Surgeon from 1855 to 1857 and who later served as Assistant Surgeon General of the Confederate Army. White told me that she had two sketches her father had made of the cantonment, and she sent copies of the sketches to me in Lubbock.

We maintained a correspondence for several years, and in some of her letters, White recalled stories told by her mother and father about life at Cantonment Burgwin, including the surprising fact that her mother had brought a piano from St. Louis to the cantonment and, while living there, played it regularly. White informed me that she had a journal kept by her father while he was at Cantonment Burgwin. She later loaned the journal to me but asked that I not publish any of the material. As it turned out, except for an occasional mention of Kit Carson and a few other prominent individuals in the Taos area, the journal was not very informative about life at the post, and it remains unpublished.

Anderson was a well-educated, curious, and talented man. He compiled bird and old Indian pottery collections, which he sent to the Smithsonian Institution. He was also an excellent artist and a careful draftsman. His drawings proved to be extremely useful in the study and reconstruction of Cantonment Burgwin. One sketch (Figure 4) was a scene looking across the parade ground toward two small buildings. It showed that most of the walls were constructed of upright logs and that these buildings had rectangular, four-paned windows and flat roofs. I could also see that parts of the walls were made of stone or adobe; these, I later learned, were the chimneys for the fireplaces.

Figure 4.

Drawing by W. W. Anderson of the buildings of Cantonment Burgwin. Anderson was Post Surgeon at the cantonment between 1855 and 1857. Note the vertical-log walls, stone or adobe chimneys, flat roofs, and window sizes and positions.

Picture courtesy of Mrs. Virginia S. White, daughter of W. W. Anderson, and her family and heirs in Sumter, South Carolina.

The other Anderson drawing (Figure 5) was even more important, at least initially. It was a scene drawn from a hill south of the cantonment, with the buildings of the post in the middle ground and the lower valley and the Taos Mountains in the distance. Because of his precise draftsmanship, I realized that I might be able to find the place where Anderson had stood when he had drawn the picture. Moreover, I knew that with this drawing, I would be able to locate the exact position of the cantonment and many of its buildings.

A few days after receiving the Anderson drawings, I drove out to Taos and climbed up the hill where I thought Anderson had been standing when he had made the sketch. It was about a half-mile south of where Rounds and I had found what we thought were traces of the cantonment. Anderson's drawing showed two easily identified ranges of hills and mountains in the distance. By moving up or down the hill, and then from side to side until I could see the hills in the exact same spatial relationship as shown on the drawing, I was able to find where Anderson had been standing. Holding the sketch up to match the scene below, I noted the sagebrush flat where Rounds and I had found traces of

Figure 5.

Drawing by W. W. Anderson looking north down the valley of the Little Rio Grande. Note the buildings of Cantonment Burgwin on the floor of the valley in the middle distance. There were more than two hundred soldiers and officers at the cantonment when this drawing was made.

Picture courtesy of Mrs. Virginia S. White, daughter of W. W. Anderson, and her family and heirs in Sumter, South Carolina.

old structures, and there on the Anderson drawing were the main buildings of Cantonment Burgwin in this same place (Figure 6).

It was a great relief to learn that the remains of the post were not under the sawmill. I immediately telephoned Rounds with the good news, and he again urged me to prepare a proposal, which I did, sending it to him in late November 1956.

The Plan to Excavate Cantonment Burgwin

The proposal I sent to Rounds clearly indicates that I was still thinking like an archaeologist with a museum background. The first two pages were devoted

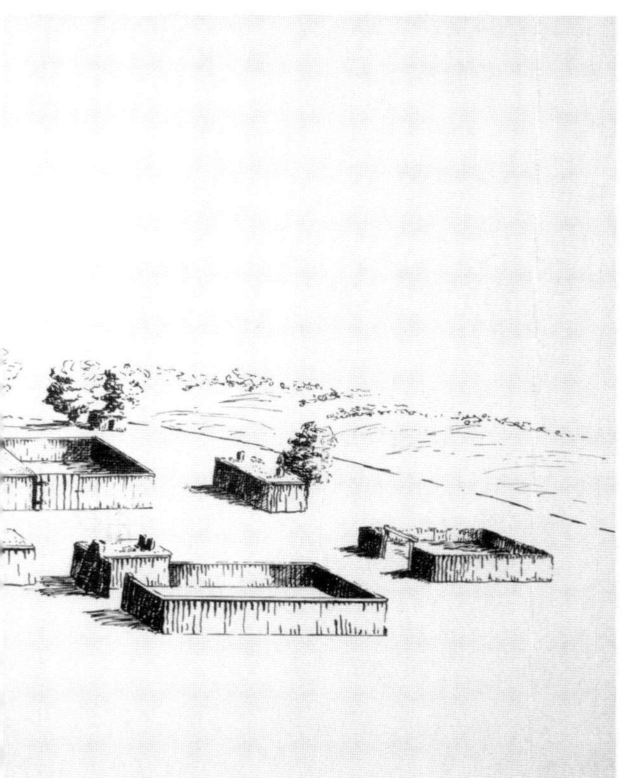

Figure 6.
Drawing based on Anderson's sketch of Cantonment Burgwin. This 1960 drawing was done by an unknown staff artist at the Museum of New Mexico Laboratory of Anthropology.

Courtesy of SMU-in-Taos.

almost entirely to a summary of the prehistoric archaeology of northern New Mexico. Only at the bottom of the second page do I begin discussing Cantonment Burgwin. I outlined what I had learned from my historical research, particularly the information from Bennett, in *Forts and Forays,* indicating that Cantonment Burgwin was built of adobe and the conflicting information from the Anderson drawings showing that the walls were made of upright logs. I was skeptical of Bennett's description, despite his participation in the construction, because the editors who published the diary noted that Bennett had written the diary, from notes, much later in life and that they had found several errors. The editors also confessed that they had done "some rearranging" of the text. I concluded that the description of the construction of Cantonment Burgwin might have been one of those editorial changes. Also, I thought the debris mounds in the sagebrush flat were not large enough to be collapsed adobe walls. I told Rounds that these discrepancies would be resolved by excavation, which would also provide the accurate information we needed to reconstruct the buildings.

I proposed to first excavate and restore the rectangular compound, which according to the Mansfield map had been used for the enlisted men's quarters and the stables. Depending on the size of the structure, I thought it could become a museum, and I outlined the general topics that might be covered in the displays. In developing this plan, I was greatly helped by my mentor at Texas Tech, W. Curry Holden, Director of the Texas Tech Museum. I cannot recall who initially suggested that a museum be built, nor can I remember when it was first discussed, but I think it was Rounds who brought it up during our meeting after the discovery of the cantonment. Whoever suggested it first, Rounds came to envision the proposed museum as the intellectual focus of the developments we planned for the area, including research facilities for scholars in a variety of fields. As the associate director of the Texas Tech Museum and a committed research archaeologist, I was certainly amenable.

A major section in the proposal was devoted to the suggested museum. I indicated that to create a museum, we would need to do more than just construct a building. We would have to bring in artists, exhibit preparators, and a staff to manage the collections. I offered the assistance of the Texas Tech Museum in arranging for these services, possibly under a management contract with Rounds's Wichita Foundation (later the Rounds Foundation). I also suggested that the facility sponsor conferences to stimulate interest in the research potential of northern New Mexico. Finally, I recommended that an endowment be established to cover the costs of maintenance and staff for the museum.

Another major section in the proposal concerned the field school. Support for the field school was perhaps my most important goal, and at this point I was proposing to excavate the cantonment and perhaps generally supervise its reconstruction in exchange for Rounds's support of the field school. My eventual role in managing the kind of facility that Rounds was visualizing was not discussed in the proposal, and I do not recall anticipating that I would become the director of the museum or the manager of the facility once it was established. My commitment was to do archaeological research.

The final section of the proposal concerned the budget. Rounds had told me that he was prepared to invest $10,000 a year in the project, so I proposed a five-year development program of that magnitude, of which $2,000 per year was to be spent on the field school and related activities. Even then, I am sure I realized that this sum was inadequate for the restoration of Cantonment Burgwin, at least at the pace indicated in the proposal. But I made a major mistake in not discussing this explicitly in the proposal. Perhaps I thought my comments in the text about arrangements for a staff to install and operate the museum were sufficient warning that a $10,000 annual investment would not be adequate to achieve the goals envisioned by Rounds. Or, more likely, I was concerned that he would abandon the project if it cost more than he was prepared to commit. As it turned out, Rounds did provide more.

Looking back, I can see that a number of issues were not addressed in the proposal—perhaps the most important being my plan for reconstructing the first building. Originally, I had thought I would hire a local building contractor in Taos to build it. However, Holden pointed out to me that from the indicated size of the building, no contractor would do the job for the money in the budget. He suggested that I hire a crew and build it myself. He also suggested that since the original walls were almost certainly made of upright logs that were not suitable for a permanent structure, I should use adobe bricks in the reconstruction of the building. Holden went on to suggest that I lay three horizontal courses of 2x12-inch boards in the adobe walls, one at the bottom, another in the center, and the third just below the concrete bonding beam at the top. These three courses of planks would permit me to attach split logs to the wall exteriors to simulate the appearance of the original vertical log walls. It was a good plan.

There is a little personal background to Holden's suggestion. When I had first arrived in Lubbock, he had persuaded me to buy an old adobe house on the outskirts of town and to add to the original building, even though I knew almost nothing about house construction, adobe or otherwise. That effort was still under way when the proposal was being written, and I was very unsure of my ability as a builder, which is probably why I did not discuss how I would actually reconstruct the building. Holden, however, felt sure that I could do it, and he repeatedly urged me to take on the job of rebuilding at least the main building at Cantonment Burgwin.

In the spring of 1957, Rounds came to visit me in Lubbock and found me hard at work, with a crew, adding two rooms to my adobe home. We had a brief discussion about my proposal, and he asked me how much reconstruction I thought I could do for the $8,000 in my budget. I told him I really did not know because there was still considerable doubt about the size of the structure, but I intended to build until I ran out of money. During this meeting I told him that I planned to personally supervise the construction of the museum, using adobe bricks and fastening split logs to simulate the exterior appearance of the building. He liked the plans, but I could tell he was concerned about my lack of building experience, even as he looked around the work under way on my house—or possibly *because* of what he saw when he looked around. Nevertheless, he said that he would increase the total amount of his gift to $20,000 each year and added that, if possible, I should try to at least get the walls up and the roof on the building that summer. I agreed, and then I asked him if he would arrange for windows to be built to my specifications, for Pot Creek Lumber Company loggers to cut the roof *vigas* for the building (*vigas*, the horizontal beams that support the roof in adobe construction, are usually almost straight logs with the bark removed and are from 10 to 14 inches in diameter), and for the company also to supply whatever lumber was needed at wholesale price. He agreed to do so. A few days later the West Texas Museum Association (the office that handled all non-state funds obtained by Texas Tech Museum) received a check for $20,000 from the Wichita Foundation, which Rounds had created to support the advancement of science.

Later that spring I received a call from George Lavender's wife, Lorraine, also an old friend of mine and coincidentally the business manager for the Pot Creek Lumber Company. She confirmed that I could expect the help I needed from the sawmill and that she and Winton Bernardin, the manager of the Pot Creek sawmill, had arranged for a shallow well to be drilled so that we would have water at the site for drinking and construction purposes. They had also made arrangements for us to use the abandoned and somewhat decrepit Pot Creek School and its kitchen to house and feed the student participants in the field school. We would need bathing facilities, however, and for that I borrowed a tent from the Texas Tech Museum and put it up near our new well. We ran a hose from the tent to the faucet that had been set up at the well, put down a few boards to stand on, and all was ready for our showers (of very cold water!) and for the excavations to begin at Cantonment Burgwin.

The First Archaeological Excavations

The archaeology field school opened on June 10, 1957, and continued for five and a half weeks; there were eleven students from six colleges and universities. Work began by clearing the sagebrush; then, with the help of the Mansfield map and the Anderson drawings, we identified all of the major structures of the post. We started to excavate the building that we had identified as the enlisted men's quarters and the adjoining stables. Almost immediately, it was confirmed that the walls were of vertical pine logs (from 12 to 14 inches in diameter, with bark intact), set in deep trenches and chinked with mud. In most cases the walls were identified by the presence of only the ghost of the bark, because the core of the logs had decayed and disappeared completely. Finding and following these walls proved to be a challenge for both the students and me (Figure 7). The interiors of the walls had been plastered with micaceous clay, available locally and known as *tierra blanca*, traces of which occurred as a minute lip on the floor along the walls in almost every room. The floors were made of leveled and packed earth (Figures 8 and 9). From the areas of broken window glass encountered in the excavations, I determined the size, number, and locations of the windows and ordered specially made windows and frames of that size. At the same time, I asked Bernardin to arrange for *vigas* of the proper length and size to be cut and brought to the building site, where they could be peeled, cleaned, and set up to dry.

Figure 7.

Excavation of the enlisted men's quarters at Cantonment Burgwin.
The view is looking west-northwest, with a bakery oven in the corner.
Note the wall traces of upright logs set in deep trenches.

Photo by Fred Wendorf.

Figure 8.

Excavation of the tack and blacksmith area, the eastern wing of the enlisted men's quarters.

Photo by Fred Wendorf.

Figure 9.

Excavated double-hearth dining room (on left) and kitchen (on right).

Photo by Fred Wendorf.

After the walls had been located and the building outlined, and with the guidance of State Representative Louis A. (Bish) Trujillo (Figure 10), who was during most of the year the yard superintendent at the sawmill, six laborers were employed to assist with the work. Being young men in their twenties and very hard workers, they and the students needed only four weeks to clear the walls, fireplaces, and floors of the entire 80-by-100-foot building (with a 40-by-60-foot interior open courtyard) that had been the enlisted men's quarters. Work was then shifted to Pot Creek Pueblo, where several test pits were dug and two rooms were excavated. The test pits showed that there had been at least two occupations and that there were pithouses below the pueblo.

The field school involved more than excavating, mapping, and recording. We were also privileged to hear lectures by four distinguished archaeologists and a physicist whom I had persuaded to come for a visit: Alex Krieger, from

Figure 10.

Louis A. (Bish) Trujillo (center), C. B. Trujillo (left), and Eloy D. Trujillo (right), ca. 1958.

Photo courtesy of C. B. Trujillo.

the University of Texas; Harold Cressman, from the University of Oregon; E. N. Ferdon and Stewart Peckham, from the Museum of New Mexico; and Norris E. Bradbury, the longtime director of the Los Alamos Scientific Laboratory and a close friend of mine. Bradbury's high-school-age son, John, had worked one summer as my assistant on several highway archaeological projects. At the field school, Bradbury discussed the application of physics to archaeology, particularly the then recently developed technique of radiometric dating.

Rebuilding the Enlisted Men's Quarters

As soon as the stable area had been cleared, about three weeks into the field school, I calculated that we would need 36,000 adobe bricks to rebuild the quadrangle of the enlisted men's quarters. Again with the assistance of Trujillo, I hired a local Taos family to make the bricks, using the dirt removed during the excavation of the stable area (Figure 11). Our plan was to erect a permanent structure to house and protect the proposed museum and research facilities. In addition, we had decided to make the outside surface of the museum approximate the original: the exterior walls would closely resemble the original vertical-log-walled building. But the inside would have modern facilities, including plumbing, heating, electricity, and permanent floors. By this time we were referring to the new facility as "Fort Burgwin" to signify its change of status from a temporary ("cantonment") to a permanent ("fort") facility.

While the excavations of the enlisted men's quarters were still under way, I found a heating and plumbing contractor and a local builder who would pour the concrete foundations and floors. My efforts to find an electrical contractor at a reasonable price were not successful. I was not overly concerned, however, because using a Sears, Roebuck "How to Wire a House" book, I had learned how to do simple wiring when I had added on to my house outside Lubbock. I thought I could wire the Fort Burgwin building myself, if necessary.

As soon as the field school was over, we began the reconstruction of the main quadrangle, using the six laborers previously employed and two students who had elected to stay and help with the work. We dug deep footings following

Figure 11.

Making 36,000 adobe blocks using the dirt from the stable area.
All the bricks were used for the reconstruction of the enlisted men's quarters.

Photo by Fred Wendorf.

the original alignment of the walls. The contractor installed heating ducts and plumbing pipes, and the builder poured the steel-reinforced concrete foundations and floors (5,600 square feet). Our arrangement with him was that we would install the reinforcing steel, he would pour the concrete foundations and floors, and we would be responsible for finishing the concrete. Unfortunately, none of us knew anything about finishing concrete, and on top of that, it was an unusually wet summer. The floors were poured each day for ten days in sections ranging in size from 400 to 800 square feet, and as luck would have it, no sooner would we finish the floor for that day than a rainstorm would come up and ruin the smooth surface of the floor. We would then have to refinish that section, sometimes two or three times as new storms appeared, one after another over the course of the afternoon. We learned a lot about concrete floor finishing, all of which I hope someday to forget. We finally finished the floors, and as soon as the concrete floors had "set," we erected the exterior walls and capped them with a steel-reinforced concrete bond beam.

I had a great deal of help during this period from Ben Gonzales, who operated La Lomita, a small, now-extinct bar and café in Taos. Ben's wife, Isabell Gonzales, was the cook, and she made the best enchiladas in Taos. My two students and I ate her enchiladas almost every night. Ben had once been a building contractor, and each evening over a beer I would tell Ben what we had accomplished during the day, and then I would ask him, "What do I do tomorrow?" Somehow, with a bit of help from Ben, we managed to put up the building.

Rounds and his wife came out in mid-August to see how the construction was going. He looked around and was delighted at what he saw. The walls were up, and we had almost completed placing the *vigas* to hold up the roof. He could see that we would probably finish on schedule (in two weeks I had to begin teaching my classes in Lubbock). He asked how the expenses were going, and I said that we would be close but that I thought we would be within budget. He told me that if I needed more money, to let him know.

The only real crisis occurred when we started to lay the ceiling deck above the *vigas* and I realized that the electrical wiring would have to be placed before we could lay the insulation and put on the roof. A quick recheck of the local electrical contractors failed to find anyone who would do the job at something less than I thought he would need to send his kids to college, and so I decided to do it myself. I laid out the twenty-six electrical circuits that I thought would be needed for the museum, being careful to keep the number of outlets on each circuit well below that required by the national electrical code. I then went to Santa Fe and purchased the necessary supplies and installed the complete system. We proceeded with the insulation and the framing for the roof, and then I called the Kit Carson Electric Cooperative to hook us up and turn on the electricity.

On arriving, the first thing the Kit Carson crew said was, "Where is your tag?" When I replied, "What tag?," they explained that in New Mexico, unlike in Texas, only a licensed electrician could install wiring, even in rural areas, and that the electrician would attach an official tag to confirm that the work had been done properly. They suggested that I check with the State Electrical Board in Albuquerque to see what could be done.

I went to Albuquerque that day and met with the supervisor of the office for the State Electrical Board. I did the only thing I could do: I told him the truth, the whole story, including my experience in Texas, and described what I had done. After asking me a few questions, he handed me a thick book and told me to read it and to come back the following week to take an electrician's licensing examination. When I showed up the following week, he asked me if I had read the book. I said yes, and he handed me a tag, saying, "Listen, young man, don't ever do that again, because this is the last tag you will ever get."

Much relieved, I returned to Fort Burgwin, hung my tag, and again called Kit Carson Electric. The same men came out, and with broad smiles they turned on the electricity. There were no flashes of light or dead wires. I had done it right.

A local contractor then installed an asphalt and gravel roof. Finally, the windows and the doors were hung and the locks installed. I had two days before I had to be back in Lubbock, and at this point, I had $230 left in the bank. The reconstruction had cost $2.30 per square foot.

Although the building was protected from the elements until the following summer, much remained to be done. The exterior needed to be stuccoed with cement, and the interior needed to be plastered and painted to match the *tierra blanca* of the original walls. Lighting and plumbing fixtures would have to be installed, water and sewer lines laid, septic tanks constructed, and partitions erected. However, the building would be safe over the winter, and with a few of the improvements noted above, my family and the students in the field school could live there the next summer (Figures 12 and 13).

Looking back, I realize that it was probably foolish of me to undertake the construction of the new facilities at Fort Burgwin. I obviously lacked the experi-

Figure 12.

The completed reconstruction of the enlisted men's quarters as seen at the end of October 1957.

Photo by Fred Wendorf.

ence to do the job well, and the construction diverted me from undertaking the archaeology that I enjoyed and for which I was trained. The energy and time I devoted to the construction kept me from promptly publishing a report on the excavations of Cantonment Burgwin, and I eventually delegated to others the publication of all of the archaeological work that we would do at the Fort Burgwin Research Center. This did, however, help the students who prepared those reports, because I insisted that the Research Center begin a publication series to document the research done under its auspices and sponsorship. Those publications were a great benefit to the careers of the students who prepared the reports. As was appropriate, we published the reports under their authorship.

There is no doubt that the success of that first effort solidified my relationship with Rounds. In the summer of 1958 he offered me a partnership in the development of the Rancho del Rio Grande Grant: he would provide the financing, and we would share equally in the profits. It might have been a profitable financial opportunity for me, but I declined. As I told him, it would be a full-time job, and I would cease being an archaeologist. He then asked me, "Since you evidently do not want to be rich, what do you want?" I responded that I wanted him to endow the research center we were building.

1958 Field School

Again sponsored by Texas Tech, the 1958 field school enrolled twelve students from five universities. They were all exceptionally hard workers, and with the

Figure 13.

Courtyard of the enlisted men's quarters today.

Photo by Fred Wendorf.

help of six local laborers, they excavated eight more rooms at Pot Creek Pueblo, cleared three deep pithouses in two different sites, dug the officers quarters at the cantonment, and tested the post hospital.

By the beginning of the 1958 field season we were referring to the new and planned facilities as the Fort Burgwin Museum and Research Center. At Rounds's request, however, there was a shift in emphasis toward research; and our new long-range plan called for a half-dozen of the smaller buildings of the cantonment (the officers' quarters and storage buildings) to be excavated and restored as quickly as possible to serve as summer homes for a research staff who would represent diverse scientific disciplines (geology, botany, zoology, and ethnology were among those mentioned, in addition to archaeology). Laboratories were to be built in the southern and eastern sections of the enlisted men's quarters and in the stable area. It was thought that these facilities, together with small stipends for the scholars and the natural attractions of the Rancho del Rio Grande Grant, would be adequate to bring outstanding scholars to Fort Burgwin to work on problems related to the Taos area. A museum was still planned, but its development was postponed. It was our plan to use the building shell that had been erected in the summer of 1957 to house my family and the students during the summer of 1958. Work began in early June 1958, when I hired a carpenter to build partitions, countertops, and cabinets in what later became our pollen lab and the public toilets. At the same time, the plumber put in a septic tank and distribution field, ran a water line from the pump house to the main building, and put in sinks and toilet fixtures. A kitchen was set up with a sink, stove, and refrigerator. All of this was still under way when my family and the students arrived on June 7. The kitchen and toilets were usable, however, and we hired Florida Archuleta to be our cook, a position she continued to hold every summer until 1993, when she retired. After the crew had settled in, I discovered that two of the laborers had some experience with plastering; I had them put the wire and stucco on the exterior of the building, and then they plastered the interior walls. While the plastering was going on, all of us had to move our beds each night to keep ahead of the plasterers. We spent $11,687.82 that year on the project, of which about 40 percent was for research. The rest went to complete the restoration and to purchase the equipment for the kitchen.

Research at Fort Burgwin

In August 1958 I received a grant from the National Science Foundation (NSF) to conduct an interdisciplinary study of the Late Pleistocene of the High Plains of eastern New Mexico and western Texas—an area known as the Llano Estacado (or "Staked Plains"). One of the flattest large areas on earth, it is dotted with several thousand fossil lake basins filled with lake sediments. The grant was sponsored by the Fort Burgwin Research Center.

In July 1956, I had shown some of the old lake basins to Kathryn Clisby, a fossil pollen specialist at Oberlin College. She and her colleague Paul Sears had initiated pollen studies in the United States. In Europe, the study of fossil pollen (palynology) had been under way for twenty years or more, but in the United States, palynology was relatively new, and Clisby was one of the pioneers in the field. She specialized in the development of pollen-extraction techniques in arid environments.

After Clisby's visit to the lake basins, both she and Sears urged me to undertake the study of Late Pleistocene environments on the Llano Estacado, with an emphasis on the study of the fossil pollen, and to seek a grant from the NSF to fund the project. The project would include hiring an experienced European palynologist to do the pollen work. Clisby was particularly insistent, calling me several times from Oberlin to ask if I had written the proposal and hounding me until I finally sat down and wrote it.

Getting down to writing the proposal took longer than it should have, since I was busy learning a new job at Texas Tech Museum. However, I appreciated the support I received from Clisby and Sears, because I was interested in paleoenvironmental studies. I also thought that such a research program at Fort Burgwin would be a way to develop interaction between scholars in several disciplines, obviously a considerable advantage for Fort Burgwin considering its limited research resources. At that time, the reconstruction of the vegetation history of an area through the recovery of fossil pollen was a new, highly promising, and relatively inexpensive technique for such studies.

Return to Santa Fe and the Museum of New Mexico

In September 1958, I accepted an appointment as Director of Research and Associate Director of the Museum of New Mexico and returned to Santa Fe. In this position, I was responsible for two of the main units of the museum: the Palace of the Governors and the Laboratory of Anthropology, as well as the State Archaeological Monuments (Figure 14). At the beginning of the summer, the financial records for the Fort Burgwin project were transferred from the West Texas Museum Association to the School of American Research in Santa Fe, which at that time managed the financial affairs of the Museum of New Mexico.

As a consequence of my change in employment, I would no longer be able to participate personally in the construction of the buildings at Fort Burgwin. I would generally supervise the construction, but I would not help lay the adobes; that would be done by contractors.

When the NSF grant was received, I hired a superbly trained palynologist from Norway, Ulf Hafsten. I also hired Earl Green, a curator at the Texas Tech Museum, to be the field foreman, geologist, and stratigrapher. Fieldwork began in the spring of 1959. During the summer, Hafsten set up a pollen laboratory in one wing of the main building at Fort Burgwin, in an area that had been our kitchen during the previous summer. His study produced spectacular results indicating that pine-spruce forests or woodlands had existed on the Llano Estacado during the Last Glacial maximum, between 22,000 and 17,000 years ago.

The report for Fort Burgwin for the third fiscal year, which began on November 1, 1958, referred for the first time to "The Fort Burgwin Research Center." The name reflected Rounds's and my desire to emphasize scientific

Figure 14.

Fred Wendorf in front of the Laboratory of Anthropology, Museum of New Mexico, 1958.

Photographer unknown. Photo courtesy of the Palace of the Governors (MNM/DCA), negative no. 42672.

research in the new facility. The major activities at the Center during the summer of 1959, however, continued to focus on the development of the facilities and on the archaeological excavations. The most important of the new facilities was the commandant's house, reconstructed by a local contractor on the footings of the original building, which had been excavated during the summer of

1958. It was intended that a full-time curator would occupy the house sometime in the future. Elsewhere, split logs were attached to the exterior walls of the main building (the former enlisted men's quarters), giving the structure an appearance similar to that of the original cantonment (Figure 13). The interior walls were painted, and an asphalt tile floor was installed. Landscaping was

Figure 15.

Aerial view of the Pot Creek Logging and Lumber Company sawmill in full operation, 1958. Note the reconstructed enlisted men's quarters on the left edge of the photograph.

Photographer unknown. Photo courtesy of the Palace of the Governors (MNM/DCA), negative no. 155888.

also begun, several dozen trees were planted to begin an arboretum, and graveled driveways and walks were built. Fort Burgwin is now a prominent feature on the landscape (Figure 15). A local man from Ranchos de Taos, Toribio Mondragon, had been employed as custodian, beginning work on April 1, 1959. Mondragon planted the trees, including the beautiful cottonwoods and willows that still line the driveway around the fort. He watered them every day from a barrel in the back of his pickup. To this day, I cannot drive along that road and see those trees without thinking of Toby and the driveway. In my own mind, I have named the driveway "Toribio Mondragon Avenue."

There was no formal field school during the summer of 1959. The archaeological excavations were done by local laborers, supervised by graduate students with previous field experience, a procedure that I would follow in my archaeological research for several years. It was an excellent arrangement because in most cases, the students could supervise a field crew with minimum oversight by me, and this greatly expanded the research that could be done; in many instances, the students could and did write the reports on their work for publication. The progress of the excavations was also greatly accelerated by a gift, from the Pot Creek sawmill, of a backhoe and front-end loader. From the surplus sales of the New Mexico Highway Department, I acquired a 1949 dump truck and a 1953 pickup. In addition to me, five graduate students from four universities participated in the 1959 archaeological excavations. Under my general direction, the excavations at Pot Creek Pueblo were supervised by Ronald Wetherington, then about to begin graduate school at the University of Michigan. In the summer of 1959, he dug twenty-five rooms (Figure 16). Other students excavated three pithouses at a village located about three miles north of the Pot Creek Pueblo (Figure 17). At the cantonment, the large building at the west end of the parade ground was excavated. This structure, with two large and three small apartments, was built after the Mansfield map had been drawn in 1853. Though its exact function is unknown, it was probably additional officers' quarters (Figure 18).

In late August 1959, the Fort Burgwin Research Center hosted the Pecos Conference, an annual gathering of most of the archaeologists working in the American Southwest. Because of the widespread interest among southwestern

Figure 16.

Excavations at Pot Creek Pueblo, 1960. Note the basins with a post in the center. These basins and center roof supports occur in most rooms.

Photo by Fred Wendorf.

archaeologists in what was happening at the Research Center, attendance at the conference was unusually large and even included several archaeologists working in areas beyond the Southwest. On one evening the Center hosted a Hispanic dinner, with entertainment that included dancers from Taos Pueblo and local Hispanic singers, guitar players, and flamenco dancers.

The Wichita Foundation gave $25,000 for the 1959 program. Slightly less than half was spent on the reconstruction of the commandant's house and the

Figure 17.

Excavation of a deep pithouse at Site TA 20. Note the burials on the floor and the heavy rocks on top of the skeletons (evidence of hostilities?).

Photo by Fred Wendorf.

Figure 18.

Reconstructed officers' quarters at the west end of the parade ground, ca. 1963.

Photo by Ron Wetherington. Photo courtesy of Taos News.

rest on the exterior split logs, painting, and installation of the asphalt floors in the main building. The archaeological research cost about one-fifth of the budget, all for labor and student fellowships. Other expenses included vehicle maintenance fuel, landscaping, a part-time custodian, and utilities.

During the summer of 1959, the Fort Burgwin Research Center was formally designated a division of the Wichita Foundation, and a nine-member Board of Trustees was appointed to establish policy and oversee operations. The officers were Ralph Rounds, President; Judge Oliver Seth, of Santa Fe, Vice President; Jack Brandenburg, Treasurer (Figure 19); and Marian Meyers, Secretary. Brandenburg, a leading member of the Taos community, was the president of the First State Bank of Taos; Meyers was Rounds's administrative assistant. Other trustees were W. J. Keller, Chief Engineer for the New Mexico District of the Federal Bureau of Public Roads (Figure 20); C. O. Erwin, Chief Engineer and Head of the New Mexico State Highway Department (both Keller and Erwin had been key people in helping my development of the

Figure 19.
J. P. (Jack) Brandenburg, February 1958.

Photo by Dorothy Brandenburg. Photo courtesy of Barbara Brenner, Taos, New Mexico.

Figure 20.
W. J. (Spike) Keller, ca. 1965.

Photographer unknown. Photo courtesy of the Palace of the Governors (MNM/DCA), negative no. 7603.

Figure 21.

Ralph C. (Bill) Rounds.

Photographer unknown. Photo courtesy of Robert Rounds.

Figure 22.

Dwight M. Rounds.

Photographer unknown. Copy by Firelock Imaging, Medford, Oregon. Photo courtesy of Becky and Cally Vickers of Medford, Oregon.

first highway archaeological salvage project and later in persuading Congress to make the project a national program); Stephan A. Mitchell, a retired attorney living in Taos and former Chairman of the Democratic National Committee; Erik K. Reed, Regional Archaeologist for the National Park Service; C. A. Nelson, Treasurer of the Wichita Foundation; and Rounds's sons Ralph C. (Bill) Rounds (Figure 21) and Dwight M. Rounds (Figure 22), both of Wichita. At some point during that first meeting of the board, I must have been appointed as the director of the Fort Burgwin Research Center. I do not have notes on when that occurred, but in the next annual report to the board, I listed myself as the director.

I had urged Rounds to appoint such a board, and he had asked me to help in nominating the initial slate of trustees. The Fort Burgwin Research Center

Board was structured to include representation from the Rounds family as well as some of the most influential citizens of the Taos and Santa Fe areas. It was a very strong and diverse board. I had worked with most of the members in the past and felt that they would be a powerful force for the future development of the Center. They were not, however, people of great wealth who might be major benefactors.

The first meeting of the Board was held at the Research Center on August 25, 1959. One of its first actions was to establish a permanent endowment for the Fort Burgwin Research Center through an initial contribution by Rounds of one thousand shares of Atchison, Topeka and Santa Fe Railway stock. In the report given to the Board of Trustees at this first meeting, I outlined in some detail a rather ambitious program for the Research Center. I proposed that the Center begin seeking scholars, in a variety of fields, who might do research at Fort Burgwin. I suggested that the Center begin by preparing a brochure to solicit proposals for projects related to northern New Mexico and by sending copies of the brochure to selected individuals with established reputations as scholars in their fields. I further proposed that the Board adopt a general theme around which the various projects could be integrated: "The history of human occupation of northern New Mexico, including the environmental factors that affected this occupation." I suggested that an advisory panel be appointed to review the proposals and make recommendations to the Board. I also urged that the Center initiate an active publication program to disseminate, to scholars and the general public, the results of research done at the Center. I suggested that the Research Center issue anthologies of papers that were based on research supported by the Center but that had appeared initially in other journals.

At this point, a museum was not in the immediate future, but I urged that the Center prepare facilities to house the collections that would result from research sponsored by the Research Center, and at the same time I cautioned the Board that the proper curation of large collections would be expensive and would require a trained staff. In the proposed program for the next year, I urged that the apartment building at the west end of the parade ground be reconstructed and that partitions be erected in the main building to provide offices and laboratories to be used by the scholars working at the Research Center. The proposed budget also included funds for equipment and furniture for the offices and apartments.

We Lose Ralph Rounds

Ralph Rounds died, suddenly and unexpectedly, while visiting Fort Burgwin on July 23, 1960. He had joined my family and me for breakfast at the fort and then had walked back to his apartment over the sawmill office. A few minutes later the office staff heard him fall to the floor. They went upstairs to investigate, called an ambulance, and then came to get me. He had had a heart attack. I was with him when he had another heart attack and died, about a half hour after we had gotten him to the Taos hospital.

It was a profound loss to me personally, to Fort Burgwin, and to the goals Rounds had set for the Fort Burgwin Research Center. The Fort Burgwin Board of Trustees held its second meeting on August 24, 1960, and elected Bill Rounds as the new president. The loss of the founder did not have an immediate impact on the Center's program, however, because most of the research and construction activities for the year had already been completed when Ralph Rounds died. As it turned out, before his death, Rounds had noted in his statement to the Board that this had been one of the most productive summers thus far, with major achievements in capital improvements and in the variety of research activities.

The decision to attract scholars from several institutions to work at the Research Center had resulted in a number of new projects that were partially supported by small grants from Fort Burgwin. Among these were the following: an archaeological survey of the Taos area by Laurence Harold, a geographer at the University of Denver; the excavation of a pithouse near the Research Center by an archaeological field school led by Ralph Leubben, of Grinnell College; a geological study of the Rancho del Rio Grande Grant by Michael Loughridge, of Harvard University; and the excavation of a nineteenth-century Hispanic farmhouse in Talpa by Herbert Dick, of Trinidad College.

At the end of his project, I asked Dick to help me as the unpaid associate director of the Research Center. In exchange, I offered him research space at the fort. The ongoing excavation of Pot Creek Pueblo continued under Wetherington's supervision. He planned to use his Pot Creek Pueblo excavations for his dissertation. To support these projects, temporary dendrochronology and ceramic laboratories were set up in the newly partitioned main building. Another important development was the beginning of the research library, which was started with large gifts of books and papers from the U.S. Geological Survey, the Museum of New Mexico, the School of American Research, and the Museum of Northern Arizona.

On several occasions Rounds had expressed his hope that eventually the Fort Burgwin Research Center would be able to obtain additional funding from other sources. His intention was that the Center would interest people of significant means to join with him in the development of the Research Center; however, my tentative efforts along that line had not been successful. At this stage, the Center was regarded as Rounds's personal project, and others who might have been able to help wanted to wait to see what happened.

Since I had already received several grants from the NSF and other foundations to support my research, I thought additional support from those sources was probably the best I could do. The NSF experimental training project in salvage archaeology was my first successful effort to develop this kind of outside support for the Research Center and was the second of several crucial grants that the Center received from the NSF. These grants not only paid the full cost of the project but also included an "overhead" of 20 to 25 percent of the direct costs to help with the maintenance and utility expenses. It is highly likely that without this support from the NSF, the Fort Burgwin Research Center might not have survived.

The experimental training project in salvage archaeology brought together a group of advanced graduate students in archaeology and several high-level administrators with whom I had worked while doing salvage archaeology in the pipeline, highway, and coal-mining industries. These administrators contributed their time to give a series of lectures about the problems of salvage archaeology as seen from their corporate perspective, and when the lectures and seminars were completed, the students were able to participate in an actual salvage project involving a strip-mine area on the Navajo Reservation near Farmington, New Mexico.

In my report to the Board at its August 1960 meeting, I noted that several manuscripts based on research done at Fort Burgwin were nearing completion, and I urged that these be jointly published by the Center and the Museum of New Mexico. These manuscripts included a report on the excavations at Pot Creek Pueblo by Wetherington (his Ph.D. dissertation), a paper by Harold on his archaeological survey of the Taos area, a report on the pithouse excavations done the previous year by Larry Hammock, and the results of the salvage archaeology training project funded by the NSF.

I also had completed a report on my NSF-funded study of Late Pleistocene environments of the Llano Estacado. In several significant aspects, the Llano Estacado research had been a pioneering interdisciplinary project. Before it was completed, the scientific staff included paleontologists, geologists, archaeologists, stratigraphers, soil scientists, and specialists in fossil pollen. The results of the pollen studies were the most spectacular, but they were also highly controversial. Despite the controversy, I urged that the Research Center publish this manuscript and begin to establish a strong reputation in multidisciplinary research on the environmental changes in the arid West during the Late Pleistocene and Holocene.

In my proposal to the Board for proposed projects for 1961 (and at the request of Bill Rounds), I suggested that at least for the immediate future, no new buildings be built. Bill had asked me to make this proposal because the future financial situation of the Center was not clear. Rounds's estate would have to be probated, and the extent of the commitment by the Rounds family to the Fort Burgwin Research Center was not known.

Activities after the Death of the Founder

Another consequence of the death of Ralph Rounds was a change on the Fort Burgwin Board of Trustees. Nelson resigned in 1961 and was replaced by Paul

B. Sears, who had been a strong supporter of the Llano Estacado project. A highly regarded botanist and palynologist, Sears had recently moved to Taos. He was a former member of the NSF Board and was the past president of the American Association for the Advancement of Science.

During all the turmoil and uncertainty that followed the death of Ralph Rounds, research activities at Fort Burgwin continued to expand. Five projects were sponsored by the Research Center in 1961. These included the following: an innovative architectural survey of Spanish Colonial buildings near Taos, a project that had been suggested by Dick and was supervised by Bainbridge Bunting, of the Department of Architecture at the University of New Mexico; a study of fossil and modern pollen in the Pot Creek area by Clisby, of Oberlin College; excavations at Pot Creek Pueblo by Ernestine Green, a graduate student at the University of Arizona; and test excavations at Picuris Pueblo, supervised by Dick. The fifth project involved Lyndon Hargrave, who in the 1930s had been a pioneer in southwestern archaeology and pottery classification and had since become a nationally recognized ornithologist. Hargrave joined the Center to identify the avian bones recovered from the various archaeological excavations conducted by Fort Burgwin. In addition, he was to collect a representative sample of the birds now living in the area for comparison with the birds that had been collected by Anderson when he had lived at the cantonment as the post surgeon in the 1850s.

In May 1961, the Fort Burgwin Research Center, together with the Museum of New Mexico, issued its first technical publication: *The Paleoecology of the Llano Estacado*. In promptly making available the results of its scholarly activities, the Fort Burgwin Research Center was beginning to function as a responsible research organization. At about the same time, I submitted to the NSF a proposal, on behalf of the Center, to continue the Llano Estacado project for two years. The grant was awarded in the fall of 1961.

Operational expenses in 1961 were much higher than planned, far more than could be sustained with the Center's expected resources. In this context it is useful to note that except for the small stipends paid to the researchers, their students, and the laborers—stipends that were charged to the individual projects—the only salaried people on the payroll were Mondragon, the part-time custodian, and Archuleta, the cook. Neither Dick nor I received a salary from the Fort Burgwin Research Center. Meyers was paid in Wichita, Kansas, by Rounds and Porter Lumber Company. At Fort Burgwin, she was my part-time secretary.

More Research Activities with NSF Support

Five research projects were sponsored by Fort Burgwin in the summer of 1962. These included a continuation of my NSF-funded study of Late Pleistocene environments on the Llano Estacado. Another NSF grant was awarded to Dick to begin a major excavation program at Picuris. There were also two carryovers from the previous year: the architectural study of Spanish Colonial buildings in the Taos area, led by Bunting; and the excavation of two early pithouses near Talpa, supervised by Green. Fort Burgwin also sponsored a two-day conference on problems related to the reconstruction of past environments. The conference was organized by Jim Hester and James Schoenwetter, both staff members on the Llano Estacado project, and was attended by nineteen scholars from eleven institutions and ten professional fields.

Both the Llano Estacado and the Picuris projects involved relatively large staffs, and the laboratories and living quarters were utilized to capacity, including the Pot Creek schoolhouse, the ownership of which, together with the sawmill site, had been given to the Fort Burgwin Research Center by Ralph Rounds in his will. Because the Picuris project operated at Fort Burgwin throughout the winter, heating had to be installed in the main building and in the staff apartment building, a long-overdue improvement. I cannot remember why, but the caution that the building program be put on hold for several years had somehow disappeared from my mind. Perhaps I thought that the large research grants would continue, or perhaps I became convinced that if an institution did not grow, it would die. Whatever the reason, I suggested that the trustees consider the construction of new housing for students and also that the east wing of the stables be reconstructed for use as a darkroom, pollen laboratories, and a shop. I also proposed that the trustees begin considering how the Center might finance a special laboratory for biological research in the reconstructed hospital. However, only the new addition of the east wing of the stables was approved, along with the installation of heating in the main office, the laboratory building, and the staff apartments.

The only other change during this year was the hiring of Ben Gonzales as custodian. Gonzales, the bar and café owner in Taos, had been my advisor for the construction of the main building five years earlier, during the first summer of the field school, in 1957. He replaced Mondragon, who had to retire because of illness.

CHAPTER 2

The Nubian Project and Other Research Activity

By 1961 my job as Director of Research at the Museum of New Mexico had come together, and as a result, the Laboratory of Anthropology was humming with new projects. At my request, and with the all-important help of my friend W. J. (Spike) Keller, from the New Mexico District of the Federal Bureau of Public Roads, Senator Clinton Anderson of New Mexico had arranged for a major increase in funds for the salvage archaeology in the reservoir area behind the Navajo Dam. Senator Anderson arranged for the increase to be large enough for us to employ several crews to work at the same time in the reservoir area. Another activity was also a very large salvage project connected with the new Interstate Highway 40, between Albuquerque, New Mexico, and the Arizona state line. It seemed that every mile of that highway construction area contained at least one major archaeological site. My job also involved excavation projects on pipeline and electrical transmission right-of-ways and a new exhibit program at the Palace of the Governors. I was able to manage all of this and still give some time to the Fort Burgwin Research Center because the Laboratory of Anthropology staff was highly competent and strongly motivated and did not need a lot of close supervision. I think there were more than sixty people on the staff, including archaeologists, curators, draftsmen, secretaries, and other technical people. The staff parking area in front of the building was so full it looked like a used-car lot.

In the late fall of 1961, I read in the newspaper that the U.S. Congress had appropriated $3 million to assist in the study of the archaeology in the area to be flooded behind the new High Dam at Aswan, Egypt. After thinking about it for several days, I called J. O. Brew, my former professor at Harvard. I told him that I was interested in studying the prehistory in the area to be inundated by the Aswan Reservoir in Egypt and Sudan. This was planned to be an enormous reservoir, extending for more than 300 miles, from just south of Aswan in southern Egypt to the Third Cataract in Northern Sudan. Brew was chairman of the UNESCO committee charged with working with Egyptian and Sudanese antiquities authorities to help save the archaeology that would be flooded by the new dam.

Before I called Brew, I had discussed with Jim Hester, then working with me on the Llano Estacado project, the possibility of working on the prehistory in the Aswan Reservoir area. I had not been very enthusiastic initially about the idea, because none of us at the museum knew anything about Egyptology or the prehistoric archaeology in the Nile Valley. As Hester pointed out to me, however, no one else knew anything about the prehistory in the Nubian Nile Valley either! I suggested that he start thinking about a grant proposal.

Even though I knew that the Aswan High Dam archaeological salvage project was going to involve archaeologists from all over the world and that it would be the most important archaeological preservation effort of the last half of the twentieth century, I was still reluctant to join the project. But my call to Brew ended my hesitation over taking on another activity. As I look back, I realize that this was perhaps the most important professional decision I ever made.

Brew told me that I would have to make a commitment for two or three years and that I should prepare two grant proposals for the necessary funding, one for Egypt and one for Sudan. At the end of our conversation, and almost as an afterthought, Brew asked me if I could I get $10,000 from private sources as a contingency fund. I told him I thought that might be possible. I then called Bill Rounds and discussed the Aswan project with him, and he pledged the needed private funding. In exchange, I promised him that the final reports from our Aswan project would be jointly published by the Fort Burgwin Research Center and the Museum of New Mexico.

This decision to study the prehistoric remains along the Nile in Egypt and Sudan was a major gamble. Except in a small area north of Aswan, no one had ever found an *in situ* Paleolithic site in the Nile Valley. The few stone pieces of that age found in the valley suggested that the area was culturally backward. These were the major reasons why Brew had not been successful in recruiting someone who knew more about Old World prehistory to do the salvage work in the Aswan Reservoir. Nevertheless, I was now eager to go, because I believed that one of the major waterways of the world was bound to contain abundant archaeology and that studying that archaeology would be very interesting. Fortunately, I was right on both counts.

The two proposals were written and submitted, and despite strong objections from a few people who noted my lack of knowledge of Old World prehistory, in June 1962 I received two large grants, one from the U.S. State Department for work in Egyptian Nubia and the other from the National Science Foundation (NSF) to support the excavations in Sudanese Nubia. The two projects could be related, but they had to be financially separate. As a practical matter, the staffs in the two projects had to be separate as well. Both projects were jointly sponsored by the Museum of New Mexico and the Fort Burgwin Research Center. I quickly began recruiting staff.

My intention was to work in Nubia for only three years, but the archaeology was so interesting and working in that part of Africa posed so many opportunities and challenges that I have continued to study there until today. This change in my research interest had a profound and perhaps unfortunate impact on the Fort Burgwin Research Center. I found that I could not direct the two Nubian projects from New Mexico: I needed to be present in the field in Africa for several months at a time. Thus, between my duties at the Museum of New Mexico and those at the Nubian project, I had very little time to give to Fort Burgwin.

Separating Fort Burgwin from the Wichita Foundation

Meanwhile, there were several changes in the Fort Burgwin Research Center Board membership at the beginning of 1963. Bill Rounds resigned as President of the Board, and Steve Mitchell replaced him. Oliver Seth also resigned, having been appointed a judge in the federal district court. Two new members were elected to the Board: William Briggs, an Albuquerque attorney who represented the Rounds family's interests in New Mexico, and Bill Lippencott, Director of the Museum of International Folk Art in Santa Fe. I had only recently met Briggs; Lippencott was an old friend.

On July 2, 1963, Fort Burgwin was incorporated in the state of New Mexico as "The Fort Burgwin Research Center, Inc." As a corporation, it was separate from the Wichita Foundation, except that the treasurer of the Wichita Foundation retained custody of the Fort Burgwin Research Center Endowment Fund until 1979. Although this move clarified the administrative and fiscal structure of the Center, there was little doubt in my mind that the Rounds family had decided to reduce its support. In my files was a letter from Bill Rounds to Herb Dick, thanking him for his good suggestions for the 1963 summer program but also saying that I had received word from Rounds that there would be no contribution from the Wichita Foundation for that year.

The stress on me was beginning to tell. The most traumatic result was my divorce that summer after eighteen years of marriage to my wife Nancy. On top of that, I had two major projects under way in the Nile Valley, both with large staffs, and several widely scattered projects under way at the Museum of New Mexico. The final blow for me was the loss of financial support for Fort Burgwin from the Rounds family.

On the positive side, I anticipated that the new corporation would be more attractive to those outside donors whose help would be required if the Fort Burgwin Research Center was to continue to exist. To begin the process of gaining that help, the Board authorized a campaign to raise additional funds for the endowment. A committee was appointed to raise the needed money and to prepare a solicitation brochure, once the Internal Revenue Service had certified the tax-deductible status of the new Fort Burgwin entity.

The financial situation at Fort Burgwin was not good. The Center had two NSF grants (the Llano Estacado and the Picuris projects), but all other planned research projects were canceled. Only one activity was not canceled: the first joint meeting of the Plains and Pecos Conferences. The Board had previously authorized hosting this meeting, and the invitations had already been extended and could not be graciously rescinded. As it turned out, the meeting was a great success; it was held between September 6 and 8, with over three hundred people in attendance. Because I charged those attending a small registration fee, the cost to Fort Burgwin was negligible.

Despite the acute shortage of funds, I remained optimistic that the Fort Burgwin Research Center would survive. I continued to urge the Board to publish the reports on research that the Center had sponsored. In my opinion, prompt publication was the key to continued foundation support, and in the fall of 1963, several of these reports were completed and ready for the printer.

Led by Lippencott, several members of the Board made substantial personal contributions, totaling over $2,000. These gifts, together with the distributions from the endowment and the overhead from the NSF grants, enabled the Center to continue operations for another year. The Board indicated that it would like to pay salaries to the previously unpaid staff (Dick and me), but I urged that the financial situation was too desperate to contemplate such expenditures, and both of us continued on an unpaid basis.

Leaving the Museum of New Mexico

In my report to the Board for activities from November 1, 1963, through October 31, 1964, I urged the Board members to remember that the Fort Burgwin Research Center was an extremely valuable asset to northern New Mexico. It was a place where scholars and their student trainees could work in pleasant, relaxed surroundings on research problems of interest and concern to the people of New Mexico and adjacent areas. The Center also provided the facilities and the financial support for the diffusion of knowledge, in the broadest meaning of that term. The Center was devoted not only to the increase in knowledge but also to the spread of this knowledge to a broad audience through sponsored public lectures and scientific meetings. I also noted that although the program of the Reseach Center had traditionally included archaeology as an important research activity, the work was by no means confined to that field; the Center had supported studies in geology, biology, botany, and history.

The summer of 1964 was another traumatic time for me. While I was away in Nubia, the Museum of New Mexico Board decided that it no longer needed my services. Only after I returned to New Mexico from Egypt did I learn that I had been fired. I immediately began to search for a new job, and a few days later, through the good offices of my old friend and colleague Claude C. Albritton, then Dean of the Graduate School at Southern Methodist University (SMU) in Dallas, Texas, I was offered a position there as Professor of Anthropology.

Albritton assured me that SMU was eager for me to continue my research in Nubia and also to remain as Director of the Fort Burgwin Research Center. I learned that the university would support all of the U.S. personnel on the Nubian project, if I wanted to bring them to Dallas. When the staff returned to Santa Fe, I invited five of them—including Hester and Joel Shiner, the field directors of the Egyptian and Sudanese projects, respectively—to join me in Dallas, and they all accepted. At the same time, SMU also hired Ronald Wetherington as an assistant professor. Ron had been my assistant in the excavation of Pot Creek Pueblo and had just received his Ph.D. from the University of Michigan.

This sudden interest in anthropology on the part of SMU can best be understood in the context of other events at that time. The previous November, President John F. Kennedy had been assassinated in Dallas. The city was still in shock. City leaders were trying to rediscover the soul of the community, and they wanted to make the people of Dallas more aware of the rest of the world. Even before I contacted Albritton, SMU had decided to develop an active anthropology program, and the university administration thought that our group could help in that effort.

In mid-May 1964, a few days after everyone had returned to Santa Fe from Nubia, I moved them, together with all of our archaeological collections, to Fort Burgwin, where we could begin the analyses and report writing. We stayed at the Center until the end of August, when our collections and our entire group, including Peta, my new wife, and our daughter, Kelly, moved to Dallas.

The archaeological collections from our excavations in Nubia comprised several million pieces, mostly flaked stone but also including a small collection of pottery and almost a hundred Late Pleistocene primitive human skeletons of the general Cro Magnon type. We had been allowed to bring almost all of the collections to the United States. It was a gift from Egypt and Sudan. They had decided to use the gift of the collections to encourage foreign institutions to help with the recovery of the archaeological materials that were soon to be destroyed by the Aswan Reservoir.

Our collections were then—and still are now—incredibly important. The collections and our notes, photographs, and maps are the only surviving record of the rich variety of the prehistoric societies that had existed in an area of more than 300 miles along the Nile, dating between 500,000 and 5,000 years ago. Had there not been this enormous effort to study those sites before they were destroyed, this rich history of human development would be completely unknown. The Nubian Campaign was a wonderful opportunity for archaeology and archaeologists to save some of the world's most important heritage. And for those few months in the summer of 1964, the Fort Burgwin Research Center held one of the largest collections, if not the largest collection, of African prehistoric artifacts anywhere outside of Africa.

As noted, the collection was moved to SMU in the fall of 1964. Years later, in May 2000, SMU decided that it no longer wanted to carry the expense and the responsibility of caring for the enormous collection, and the university asked me to find a suitable home for the artifacts. A few days later (it is amazing how fast news can travel), I was contacted by Vivian Davies, Keeper of Ancient Egypt and Sudan at the British Museum, who asked me if I would be interested in placing the collection in his museum. Of course I would. The British Museum is among the most distinguished museums in the world. Arrangements were quickly made, skilled packers were sent from London, and in September 2001, everything—artifacts, maps, notes, photographs, computer printouts (an estimated 6 million pieces)—was shipped to the British Museum, where the collection is now being looked after in a fine new facility.

In the summer of 1964, in addition to the analysis of the Aswan material,

Dick's Picuris Pueblo project was also active at the Fort Burgwin Research Center. The Picuris study was supposed to be winding down that summer, and Dick had obtained a grant from the NSF to cover the costs of analysis and report writing. An emergency arose, however, when the pueblo obtained a grant to install an extensive water and sewer system requiring the excavation of many trenches in areas previously not available to the archaeologists. Dick was able to get an emergency contract from the National Park Service to do salvage archaeology in the areas to be trenched for the water and sewer lines. Important new data were recovered during the salvage project, but the schedules for the analysis and report writing were completely disrupted. As a consequence, the project staff had to spend the winter at Fort Burgwin writing their reports.

In 1964 the Research Center received yet another NSF grant for an ethnographic and linguistic study of Taos and Picuris. This grant was directed by George Trager, a famous linguist at New York University at Buffalo. However, the grant came too late for him to organize the field research that summer, and he postponed the study to the summer of 1965.

Although there was less variety than usual in the research activities at Fort Burgwin in 1964, the center managed to issue three long-overdue publications: *Taos Adobes,* an innovative study of Spanish Colonial domestic architecture, by Bainbridge Bunting, Jean Lee Booth, and William R. Sims Jr.; *The Reconstruction of Past Environments,* by Jim Hester and James Schoenwetter; and *Contributions to the Study of Nubian Prehistory,* assembled and edited by me. The publication of my Nubian report was financed by one of the State Department grants to that project and by funds committed to the Aswan project by Bill Rounds in 1962. The Fort Burgwin Research Center and Southern Methodist University Press jointly issued this Nubian volume (and also the two other volumes that would follow in 1968).

The Rounds Estate Probated

A number of changes in the Fort Burgwin Research Center Board and staff occurred during 1965. First, Dick resigned as Assistant Director of the center, after I was unable to provide the money he needed to complete his report on the excavations at Picuris Pueblo. Second, Marian Meyers resigned from the Board. She had become eligible for Social Security and, as planned, was retired by Rounds and Porter Lumber Company. She wanted to stay at Fort Burgwin, however, so I placed her on the staff of the Research Center at a small salary, far less than she was worth. She was a highly skilled secretary and at one time had been a court reporter. Meyers was then living in the commander's house at Fort Burgwin. Her presence was an important part of the security for the fort when the facilities were closed for the winter.

Other changes on the Board in 1965 included the resignation of W. J. Keller, William Briggs, Bill Rounds, and Dwight Rounds. The last three resignations probably reflected the Rounds family's decision not to continue supporting Fort Burgwin. This, at least for a time, ended the active participation of the Rounds family in the affairs of the Center. I am sure that Keller's resignation was due to his being a member of the Museum of New Mexico Board, which had fired me. As replacements, five new members were elected to the Fort Burgwin Research Center Board in 1966: George Lavender, the lumberman whose suggestion had started the Center; Ward Vickery, an oilman from Wichita, Kansas; Lewis MacNaughton, a geophysicist from Dallas; Claude Albritton, my dean at SMU; and me. Jack Brandenburg became Chairman, and I was elected President and Director. With the new appointments, there were now eleven board members. The continuing members were Brandenburg, Lippencott, Mitchell, C. O. Erwin, Erik K. Reed, and Paul B. Sears; of these, Brandenburg, Mitchell, Erwin, and Reed were the only members remaining from the original, 1959 Board.

Late in 1964 the Rounds estate was successfully probated and settled. The Rounds family had decided to sell the Rancho del Rio Grande Grant, and in a combined sale/swap arranged with the U. S. National Forest Service, the estate received cash and property, owned by the Forest Service, near Albuquerque. (With these resources, Bill and Dwight Rounds purchased a large part of the old mining camp of Breckenridge, Colorado, and began to develop it as a ski resort. At that time, I could not understand why they would give up their beautiful property near Taos for a valley full of old mine tailings. Events proved the wisdom of their decision. Breckenridge became a very successful ski area and very valuable property.) With no further tie to the Rancho del Rio Grande Grant, the Rounds family, understandably, no longer held a strong interest in Fort Burgwin.

In the purchase agreement with the Forest Service for the Rancho del Rio Grande Grant, the Rounds family did retain the lower areas in the Little Rio Grande Valley. Bill and Dwight Rounds gave the Fort Burgwin Research Center the opportunity to purchase any of these lands at the value placed on them by the Forest Service. Among the terms of Rounds's will was a bequest of $225,000 for the Fort Burgwin Research Center Endowment Fund. This bequest and the offer from the Rounds family gave Fort Burgwin a great opportunity. The Board decided that it would be in the long-term best interest of the Research Center to use approximately half of Rounds's bequest to purchase 250 acres of land surrounding the fort, for future development. This included the sawmill site and much of the area on the west (Fort Burgwin) side of the highway, including the lower footslopes of the mountain. The area extended from just south of the confluence of Pot Creek with the Little Rio Grande to beyond the hill where Post Surgeon W. W. Anderson had stood in 1856 to make the sketch of Cantonment Burgwin and the valley to the north. It was clear, however, that at least for the immediate future, no development would be undertaken.

When Ralph Rounds died, the Rounds/Lavender partnership was dissolved and the sawmill at Pot Creek was closed. Unfortunately for Fort Burgwin, however, a short-term lease had been given to Buddy Bostian, a local lumberman, for a sawmill on the site. This proved to be a major problem to Fort Burgwin as it tried to utilize its newly acquired property. Long after that lease had expired, Bostian continued to operate his sawmill, and the Center was not able to evict him completely until the end of 1968—and then only after filing suit and taking him to court.

My move to SMU brought new life to the Research Center and a shift in operational strategy. Rather than emphasizing grants from outside institutions to support research activities, I sought to attract field schools from several different institutions, charging them rent for the use of the facilities at a rate adequate to cover much of the cost of operating the Center. This change was dictated in part by SMU's requirement that it sponsor and administer my NSF grants, which deprived Fort Burgwin of the overhead those grants had been providing the Research Center. The change in operational strategy was also in response to the interest shown by several SMU faculty, as well as faculty at other institutions, in conducting field schools and classes at Fort Burgwin. Nevertheless, my decision to use field schools to support the Research Center had an unanticipated adverse impact on my role at Fort Burgwin. I became an unpaid general manager who provided housing and meals for the students and faculty in the various field schools, and I performed this job with almost no assistance. This left very little time in the summer months for me to be an archaeologist.

As a result of this change in the program, in the summer of 1965 there were three field schools at Fort Burgwin, two from SMU (one in archaeology led by Wetherington, the other in geophysics directed by Eugene Herrin) and a University of North Carolina geology field school supervised by David Dunn. In addition, Fort Burgwin sponsored three research projects. The largest of these was the excavations at Picuris Pueblo directed by Dick. Several of the people who worked on that project had spent the winter and spring at Fort Burgwin doing analysis and writing their reports. Their work was nearly completed when they moved out in late May. In my report to the Board, I indicated that Fort Burgwin, as the sponsor of the project and the administrator of the NSF and Park Service grants that supported the Picuris work, was still responsible for the publication of the report on those excavations. I urged that the Center honor this commitment, despite Dick's resignation. It was years later, however, before the reports were finished, in part because of Dick's death in 1992. After his death, the manuscripts sat in Dick's files, essentially finished but needing integrating and editing. In 1995 Dick's widow, Martha, offered the manuscripts to Mike Adler, a member of the SMU faculty and the staff archaeologist at Fort Burgwin. Adler edited and prepared the assembled report for publication, and in 1999 the Clements Center and Southern Methodist University Press published the report, with Herb Dick and Mike Adler listed as assemblers and authors.

The second active research project during the summer of 1965 was George Trager's Taos and Picuris project, supported by an NSF grant and administered by Fort Burgwin. With a group of graduate students, Trager conducted a study of Taos and Picuris languages. Trager and his students also investigated how these two pueblo societies had functioned.

The third research project supported by Fort Burgwin was a small study of fossil pollen from a Late Pleistocene profile I had sampled in Blackwater Draw, located between Clovis and Portales in eastern New Mexico. Intended as the last activity of the Llano Estacado project, the report was analyzed by Paul Sears and Edena Papazian. Unfortunately, I failed to write the final version of the report on this important locality. Eventually I gave the report to one of my former graduate students, Christopher Hill, who recently published a very interesting paper on the major results of that study.

Field Schools from Everywhere and Other Scholarly Activities

In the following year, 1966, there were six separate scholarly activities at the Center; three were field schools, but none of the field schools were from SMU. There was a geology field school from the University of North Carolina, with twenty-three students led by David Dunn; an art seminar from Texas Tech, with thirty-three students headed by Clarence Kincaid; and an archaeology field school from Northern Illinois University, with eight students directed by James Gunnerson. This last group excavated a site near Mora, on the eastern side of the mountains from Fort Burgwin. With the help of a grant from the Millicent Rogers Foundation of Taos, the Research Center also sponsored an architectural study of religious structures in the Taos area. In addition, Trager received another two-year grant from the NSF to continue his linguistic and ethnographic studies of Taos and Picuris. His wife, the linguist Dr. Felicia Trager, and four graduate students assisted him on that project.

There were also two proposed projects that did not develop but that merit comment. In my report to the Board in 1965, I had observed that we had not been very effective in reaching out to the Taos community. I suggested two activities that I thought might change this situation. The first idea was a series of public lectures by distinguished, internationally prominent scholars on recent significant scientific developments and the impact of these developments on modern life. For the summer of 1966, I arranged for Willard Libby, the discoverer of ^{14}Carbon dating and a Nobel Laureate, and Paul Sears to be the first two speakers in the series. Unfortunately, I became seriously ill during the late spring when the organizational work needed to be done, and the lectures had to be canceled. After that, and mostly because of our limited financial resources, I never again attempted to organize the distinguished lecture series.

The other proposal that I offered as an outreach to the Taos community was to install a small museum in the west wing of the main building. Although I noted that this would require resources not then available, the idea of a museum received serious attention by the Board, and I was authorized to explore how the installation might be done.

The facilities at the Center were completely full in June and July 1966, with some limited use in August. Most of the students in the field schools were housed and fed in the old schoolhouse, which by now was not really suitable for use as a dormitory. Some of the students and three of the faculty had to find housing in Taos, and there was not enough office and laboratory space. Something needed to be done, but there were no funds that could be used to construct new buildings. In this situation, my highest priority was additional housing, laboratory, and office space, and I saw an opportunity to make a personal contribution toward solving that need.

In 1965 the Board had authorized that I be paid two months' salary, but our resources were such that I did not accept payment. In 1966 the Board again authorized two months' salary for me. This time, I decided to use my budgeted salary to begin the construction of the east wing of the main building—the stable area of the cantonment. Eventually the new space could be used as laboratories and offices. Without consulting the Board, I started construction. The funds were sufficient to put in the foundations, erect the adobe walls, install the bond beam, and place the roof *vigas*. But there was not enough money for the roof, doors, or windows.

When the Board met two weeks later, I told them what I had done and why. I also told them that without a roof for the wing, the walls would soon be damaged or possibly destroyed by rain and snow, and I urged them to help me find a way to protect the building. There was total silence while the Board digested my rash behavior. From their facial expressions, I could tell that they appreciated my willingness to commit my personal funds toward the solution of one of our most pressing needs. But their facial expressions also told me that they wished I had consulted them. The silence was broken by MacNaughton. With a laugh at my brashness, he said he would contribute the funds needed to put on a roof. As soon as the meeting ended, I began installing the roof. I had only a week before I had to return for my classes at SMU. It would be several years before the building was completed, but a start had been made.

One of the casualties of putting that roof on the building was my friendship with Ben Gonzales. The roof was almost finished, but not quite, when we quit on a Friday evening. Ben refused to return on Saturday to help me finish the roof, despite the fact that rain was expected over the weekend. The roof had to be done on Saturday if I was to return to Dallas in time for my classes on the following Monday. I begged him to help me finish the roof, but he still declined. In a fit of anger, I told him not to return on Monday; he was fired. I found the men I needed to help me finish the roof by going into Taos the next morning and asking anyone standing on a street corner if they would help me for a day to install a roof. In thirty minutes I hired two good workers. We finished the roof by noon, but I paid them for the whole day. Over the years I have carried considerable guilt over my hasty action in firing Ben. We had been good friends since that first summer of 1956, but no longer. For some time, I had been considering returning to a part-time custodial staff that would be employed only during the summer months. Rather than replace Ben with another full-time custodian, I implemented that plan immediately.

There was one other important discussion with the Board during its 1966 meeting: I broached the subject of a possible merger between the Fort Burgwin Research Center and Southern Methodist University. In the fall of 1964, shortly after I had moved to SMU, Albritton and I had begun discussing the possibility of a merger. I was worn out by the constant strain of near insolvency, yet I knew that my commitment to the memory of Ralph Rounds was such that I could never leave Fort Burgwin unless its future was secure. There was considerable interest in Fort Burgwin among the faculty in several departments in the university, and I felt certain that if the Center was part of SMU and properly developed, it would become a unique and valuable asset. Albritton and I thought the idea had sufficient merit to be discussed with the Fort Burgwin Board. When we brought up the issue at the 1966 Board meeting, the discussion was generally positive, and the idea of a merger was approved in principle. The Board asked us to find out what might be arranged.

Meanwhile, the Anthropology Department at SMU continued to grow, with several new appointments. Among these were George and Felicia Trager, who moved to SMU in June 1967, further strengthening and broadening the anthropology program. The move also solidified the Tragers' ties to Fort Burgwin. Four field schools operated at the Center in the summer of 1967. Three were from SMU: an archaeology field school led by Wetherington; a linguistic field school directed by the Tragers; and a class in oil painting taught by the distinguished artist Forest Judd, of SMU's Meadows School of the Arts (Figure 23). After the linguistic field school ended in mid-July, the Tragers continued their linguistic and ethnographic research at Taos and Picuris. With a grant from the National Institute of Health, one of their former students, Dr. Estellie Smith, of Florida State University, used the Research Center as a base while she conducted an ethnographic study of Isleta Pueblo, located south of Albuquerque. Finally, the fourth field school, led by Dr. Robert Butler, was from the University of North Carolina.

The idea of a museum continued to move forward. With the urging and assistance of Curry and Fran Holden (Curry had been my boss when I was at Texas Tech in Lubbock), I developed preliminary plans and a budget for an exhibit gallery in the west wing of the enlisted men's quarters, the structure that we had named the Rounds Building.

Figure 23.

SMU Meadows School of the Arts student-artist at Fort Burgwin.

Photographer unknown. Photo courtesy of Taos News *and SMU.*

There were also two important changes in the membership of the Fort Burgwin Research Center Board of Trustees. Lippencott resigned; he had moved to California to attend graduate school in anthropology. In his place, Dwight Rounds agreed to serve again. I viewed Dwight's presence on the Board as an important element for the continuity of the Research Center, and I had urged him to rejoin us. Along with Dwight, the Board now included Jack Brandenburg, Chairman; C. O. Erwin, George Lavender, Steve Mitchell, Erik Reed, Paul Sears, Ward Vickery, Lewis MacNaughton, Claude Albritton, and myself (President and Director).

In addition to the changes on the Board, James Sciscenti, an archaeologist on the faculty at SMU, became Assistant Director of the Research Center. His help was greatly needed because the summer of 1968 would be one of the most active periods at the Center up to that time.

Planning a Merger with SMU

By the spring of 1967, Albritton and I had decided that the situation was right for us to discuss with Willis Tate, President of SMU, a possible merger between the Fort Burgwin Research Center and SMU. Tate expressed an interest in a possible merger and agreed to attend a meeting of the Fort Burgwin Research Center Board in Taos on June 24, 1967. This was a very successful meeting, with everyone seeming to agree on the main points of a possible merger.

In September, when I returned to Dallas, Tate asked Albritton and me to prepare a proposal recommending how a merger might occur. We responded with a joint memorandum, dated September 28, 1967, and suggested that he request the university legal staff draw up a draft of an agreement that would contain six main points:

1. The assets of Fort Burgwin would be transferred to SMU, with a reversionary clause.
2. SMU would manage, maintain, and augment the educational program

of the Research Center in accordance with the stipulation of the Center's founder.

3. The present Board of Trustees would be reappointed to a newly constituted Board of Overseers for Fort Burgwin, to conduct annual reviews of the program and budget of the Center, to make recommendations concerning the director and his staff, and to offer suggestions concerning new members or the reelection of current members of the Board.
4. The director of the Center would be a full-time member of the university (and for continuity, I would be reappointed Director for whatever term was agreeable to the Board of Overseers and the SMU Board of Governors).
5. All funds received from the Fort Burgwin Research Center Endowment Fund and any other gifts specified for Fort Burgwin would be dedicated solely to the programs there.
6. The annual budget of the Fort Burgwin Research Center would be carried separately on the budget of the SMU Graduate School and would be subject to the same procedures of preparation, review, and audit as any other department of the graduate school.

We also urged Tate to invite Brandenburg, Rounds, and Rounds's lawyer to meet with the SMU Board of Governors to review the draft of the agreement and to let Rounds's lawyer and SMU's legal counsel prepare the agreement for formal consideration by the two corporate parties. The memorandum to Tate was accompanied by a six-page statement of the advantages of the proposed merger with SMU and a budget sheet showing the current assets of Fort Burgwin (total, $547,000) and current financial requirements showing expenditures.

A week later, on October 6, 1967, I sent Tate a second memorandum on the goals of the Research Center, stating: "The emphasis throughout the history of the Research Center had been in the field of anthropology, broadly defined, and it is hoped that this will be maintained as an expression of the interests of the founder and donor." I added that the Research Center might be used to promote the development of any area of art or science and that the facilities could "be used for training and research in drama, art, history, or any other area where the location or type of facilities available at Fort Burgwin provide an advantage over a normal campus situation." Thus, although I expected anthropology to continue to be the major focus, I felt that the Center should not be limited to that field but should be seen as an asset for use by much of the university. I also included a revised budget, which reduced the expected income from the endowment and estimated the cost to the university.

Evidently these memoranda convinced Tate that a merger with Fort Burgwin was in the best interest of SMU, and he arranged for a draft agreement to be prepared. Unfortunately, there was no effort to involve the Rounds family's attorney, as we had recommended, and neither Albritton nor I was consulted. The proposed draft was strongly biased in favor of the university, and when it was sent to Brandenburg, he rejected it.

At Albritton's and my urging, Tate then invited Brandenburg, Rounds, Meyers, Albritton, and me to meet in his office on March 6, 1968, to discuss the proposed merger. According to the minutes of that meeting, Brandenburg explained why the preliminary draft was not acceptable: it did not include the main points that protected the interests of Fort Burgwin and that had been agreed to at the June 24, 1967, meeting. After some discussion of those concerns, Tate agreed to include those points in the merger document.

At that point I explained that for SMU to make effective use of the Research Center, the partially built laboratory and office wing of the Rounds Building would have to be finished and more dormitory space built. I went on to suggest that the transfer of Fort Burgwin's assets be done in three stages: the first would occur immediately on completion of the agreement and would consist of the transfer of half of the 70 acres of the campus, with an agreement that the laboratory and office wing would be completed within two years; the second stage would transfer the remainder of the campus on completion of a new dormitory for at least twenty students; and the third stage would occur in 1979, when the assets of the endowment fund, including the 250 acres of land adjoining the campus and purchased by the endowment for Fort Burgwin, would be transferred to SMU and restricted solely for the operation, maintenance, and capital improvements of the Fort Burgwin Research Center. Tate noted that the university did not have the funds to complete the laboratory and office wing. I told him that I thought I might be able to get most of the money needed to complete the wing through an anthropology facilities grant program at the NSF. Tate then agreed to this approach but cautioned that I would still have to find the money if the NSF proposal was rejected. Everyone understood that the merger with SMU was going to be a two-year "trial marriage"; if SMU could not raise the money to finish the laboratory building and build a dormitory, then the Research Center would revert to Fort Burgwin under the reversionary clause of the agreement.

Merger with SMU Completed

On June 30, 1968, the Fort Burgwin Research Center merged with Southern Methodist University. I recall that when Tate signed the agreement, he turned to Albritton and said: "OK, it is done. Now tell me, Claude, have I bought another one of your damn alligator farms?" That was too good a jab for me to ignore, so later that summer when I sent Tate a letter about something or other, I typed across the top as a letterhead, "Tate's Alligator Farms, Taos Division."

The formal agreement was between Southern Methodist University, the Fort Burgwin Research Center, and the Wichita Foundation, the last because it was the custodian of the Research Center's endowment fund. In Paragraph 1 of the agreement, the university agreed "to carry out within the University program, consistent with its purposes and objectives as an institution of higher learning, the purposes and objectives of Fort Burgwin, to wit: To conduct research and study in the general fields of archaeology, anthropology, history, biology, climatology and geology; to encourage such study and research; to establish and/or encourage the establishment of one or more museums for the study and display of arts and exhibits in such fields; to disseminate and make available through any medium, including publications, the results of such research and study, and research and study of other persons or organizations, and by any other means to improve the level of knowledge, education and scientific techniques."

Under the terms of the agreement, the Research Center's property and assets were to be transferred to SMU in the three steps I had proposed. The first asset—approximately half of the 70 acres designated as the Center's campus—was transferred immediately, with the final transfer, including those properties and assets held by the endowment, to occur on June 30, 1979. For the agreement to remain viable, the Fort Burgwin Research Center had to remain a corporate entity for at least twenty-one years, until June 30, 1989, in order to receive the Fort Burgwin assets should for some reason the university not fulfill the agreement. SMU was also prohibited from disposing of any of the land transferred to it during that period of twenty-one years.

As I had promised Tate in May 1968, I also prepared and submitted, in the name of SMU, a proposal to the NSF Anthropology Program for funds to finish the laboratory/office building, as required by the merger agreement.

Student Housing and Cleaning the Campus

In the summer of 1968 more students were housed at Fort Burgwin than ever before. Additional housing for students and faculty had become available when the Buddy Bostian's sawmill was finally forced to move from most of Fort Burgwin's property in the fall of 1967. Three houses occupied by sawmill workers and also the office building, all on the south bank of Pot Creek, became available to the Research Center (several shacks on the north side of the creek continued to be occupied by some of Bostian's workers until the end of 1968). The abandoned frame houses were basically sound but had been stripped of plumbing and wiring. To make them suitable for our use, we cleaned and cased the water well at each house and installed a water pump, electrical wiring, and plumbing fixtures (toilets, showers, and sinks). The downstairs of the old office building was also used as a student dormitory and the upstairs as faculty housing. We continued to use the old schoolhouse as a dormitory for the students in the geology field schools and also as a dining hall, with Florida Archuleta in charge of the kitchen and dining facilities, feeding three meals a day to sixty to seventy people. Even with the new facilities, however, two of the faculty and six of the students could not be housed at the Research Center that summer.

We charged the students only a nominal fee to live there for the period of the field school. There was no effort to develop rent income sufficient to amortize the cost of the repairs, probably because I realized that these old houses were at best a temporary solution. Most of them were really just shacks, but the students did not seem to mind. They had to work hard in the field schools, but in the dormitories they had lots of freedom to come and go as they pleased. No one worried that they might damage the buildings or the old army surplus beds and other furniture I had put in them, and everyone seemed to enjoy living there.

When Fort Burgwin took possession of the Pot Creek sawmill site, the land was littered with enormous quantities of trash of every conceivable type: old car bodies, washing machines, scrap wood, dead trees, sawmill parts, and huge piles of sawdust. The junk included just about everything that people might abandon during twenty years of living and working at a sawmill, posing a vast cleanup job, far beyond our resources. Meyers, through her contacts in the Taos community, arranged for the Mainstream Project of the Office of Economic Opportunity to employ a crew to begin the cleanup, using our trucks and other equipment and under our supervision. Working through the entire fall of 1968, they removed to the Taos landfill over three hundred truckloads of debris. They cleaned up Pot Creek, as well as most of the sawmill area south of the stream.

Seventy students in five separate training programs were housed at Fort Burgwin during the summer of 1968, including a geology field school sponsored jointly by the University of North Carolina and Georgia State University, headed by David Dunn and Robert Bently; two field schools from SMU, one in archaeology directed by James Sciscenti and Ned Woodall and another in linguistics and ethnology led by George and Felicia Trager; and a high-school-level archaeology field school directed by Jon Young and Jack Zahniser. In addition, there was an NSF-supported experimental training program in microstratigraphy. The course was taught by Achilles Gautier, from the University of Gent,

Belgium, by C. Vance Haynes, of the University of Arizona, by Claude Albritton, from SMU, and by me.

The microstratigraphy field school was unusual. The student participants consisted of sixteen carefully selected advanced graduate students from six universities. We were very fortunate in the selection of these students. Today, many of them are among the most distinguished members of the profession, including one (David Hurst Thomas) who is a member of the National Academy of Sciences (two of the faculty are also members of the Academy: Haynes and me). To conduct the course, the faculty took the students on a group tour of several Late Pleistocene "Early Man" sites in Texas, New Mexico, and Arizona. At each site the students studied the stratigraphy and drew profiles and maps. When the tour was completed, everyone returned to Fort Burgwin to write their reports, which had to be finished, including all of the drafting, before they could leave the field school. All of the participants, including the faculty, regarded the course as very challenging and a great success. The NSF urged me to apply for another grant to hold the course again, but Albritton and I found it both physically difficult and intellectually demanding. We decided once was enough. Besides, we were not sure that the next one could be as good.

The Research Center, with two grants from the Millicent Rogers Foundation in Taos, also continued to sponsor the study of Spanish colonial religious architecture in the Taos area. Two members of the Department of Architecture at the University of Colorado were employed. Unfortunately, Bainbridge Bunting had moved on to other interests, and without him, the project never seemed to have the focus that had led to the highly successful *Taos Adobes* publication.

The 1968 fiscal year did see the publication of two reports on research sponsored by the Research Center: *The Prehistory of Nubia,* in two volumes plus an atlas, assembled and edited by me and published jointly by SMU Press and the Fort Burgwin Research Center (Fort Burgwin Publication No. 5); and *The Excavation of Pot Creek Pueblo,* by Ronald Wetherington (Fort Burgwin Publication No. 6). Both were important for Fort Burgwin because they demonstrated that the Center, despite its limited resources, continued to recognize its responsibility to disseminate the information gathered on the projects it sponsored.

The Nubian volumes were also important because of the widespread public and scholarly interest in the UNESCO-sponsored Nubian Campaign. They brought the Center to the attention of a large international community.

Building the Museum in the Enlisted Men's Quarters

During the summer of 1967, Curry and Fran Holden supervised preparations for the proposed museum at Fort Burgwin: they outlined the topics to be covered, created the layout, and determined the arrangements and dimensions of the cases and panels, as well as the subjects to be addressed in each display. That fall, in September 1967, the workshop in the museum at Texas Technological University in Lubbock began construction of seventeen glass-fronted exhibit cases, fourteen wall panels, and a reception-sales desk for the Fort Burgwin museum, all under the Holdens' supervision. Fort Burgwin purchased the materials (at a favorable price arranged by Rounds and Porter Lumber Company) and paid the salary of the cabinetmaker employed by Holden. In late spring of 1968, the disassembled cases and panels were transported to the Center, and in the beginning of the summer of 1968, the exhibit cases were reassembled, equipped with interior lighting, and set in place in the exhibit hall. Shortage of funds, however, forced us to delay the installation of the exhibits until the summer of 1969.

I had arranged that the exhibits were to be installed under the supervision of Stephen Borhegyi, an old friend from Santa Fe and Director of the Milwaukee Public Museum, one of the best museums in the country. Borhegyi accomplished this by organizing a class in museum exhibit techniques and holding it at Fort Burgwin during the summer of 1969. He also developed the final text for the labels, selected the artifacts and photographs to be used in the exhibits, and supervised the students while they installed the exhibits in the new display cases. The cost of the exhibit installation was minimal—limited to providing housing for Borhegyi, his family, and the students, plus several student stipends and a few supplies. The installation proceeded very rapidly, and in a period of six weeks the exhibits in approximately half of the museum area were completed. The plan was for Borhegyi to finish the museum exhibits the following summer, but this was not to be: he died in an automobile accident a few months after returning to Milwaukee.

In addition to the museum exhibits, in 1969 Fort Burgwin built a dormitory, organized a kitchen and dining hall, published one monograph, and arranged for two other reports to be edited and readied for the printer. The Center also hosted five field schools from four different universities. The largest was in geology, with twenty-five students, and was led by David Dunn, from the University of North Carolina. Another geology field school, conducted with the University of North Carolina's field school, had eight students under the supervision of Charles Wagg, of Georgia State University. Two other field schools were sponsored by SMU: one, in archaeology and supervised by James Sciscenti, had twenty-two students; the other, in linguistics and ethnology, had fifteen students and was led by George and Felicia Trager. The fifth field school was also in archaeology. With eighteen high school students, it was led by Jack Zahniser and Jon Young, of the Catalina Island Boys School in California. This group excavated one of the small Pot Creek Pueblo units that it had tested the previous summer.

All of this became possible because Dunn, at the end of his field program in 1968, came to my office to talk about student housing at the Center. He told me that the old schoolhouse was no longer suitable as a dormitory for his students. He went on to say, however, that the University of North Carolina would be willing to sign a multiyear contract to continue staying at the Research Center if the Center would build a suitable dormitory for its students. He suggested that I use the contract to get a loan to build a new dormitory.

As Dunn and I continued our discussions about the need for a new dormitory, we walked across the highway to an area about a hundred feet south of the old sawmill office building. We stopped where there was a cement block footing that had once supported a large metal "Quonset hut" used by the sawmill as a machine shop and garage. The metal building had been removed when the Rounds and Lavender sawmill closed, leaving the footing in excellent condition and standing about four feet high. Dunn noted that the footing was about the right size and in an ideal location for a geology dormitory. He told me that he would have the rental contract prepared shortly after he returned to North Carolina, and in turn, I promised him that I would try to arrange for a loan to build the new dormitory. Meanwhile, and before he left for North Carolina, Dunn prepared some simple plans showing how he would like the interior to be arranged. He thought the new building would sleep about forty students comfortably, with space for showers and toilets, plus an area for drafting and another for storage of equipment and samples.

When I received the contract a few weeks later, I went to Albritton, who agreed to arrange for SMU to give Fort Burgwin an advance against rents sufficient to cover the cost of construction. He was delighted to do this because the new dormitory would fulfill the commitment by SMU to build a new student dormitory. When the loan was arranged, I ordered work to begin immediately on the building, and it was completed in the spring of 1969. Work was still under way on the showers and toilets when the two geology field schools occupied the building in early June. The loan was repaid in three years.

Also in the spring of 1969 we moved the kitchen and dining area from the old schoolhouse to the lower floor of the sawmill office building. There were three rooms in this lower section: in one we installed a refrigerator, stove, and sinks; in another, we placed tables and benches for the dining area; and in the third, we erected shelves so that the room could serve as a pantry. The kitchen was larger and much cleaner than the one in the old schoolhouse, but the dining area was smaller. There was room for only fifty people to sit at one time, about half the number of the students and staff who would be eating there. Archuleta solved that problem by serving two sittings at every meal.

In addition to all these building and remodeling activities, the Research Center also completed another publication. With the aid of a gift from MacNaughton, the Center finally published *Papers in Taos Archaeology* (Fort Burgwin Publication No. 7), by Laurence Herold and Ralph Leubben. In my report to the Board, I noted that three other manuscripts were ready or almost ready for the printer. Unfortunately, MacNaughton had died in late 1968. It was a great loss to Fort Burgwin. His widow, Mrs. Ina MacNaughton, had agreed to serve the remainder of his term.

At the August 6, 1969, meeting of the Board I discussed the various field school activities at the Center during that summer, and I also reported that I had begun discussions with Louis Walker, an architect in Santa Fe, to develop a long-range plan that would involve new dormitory and dining facilities for Fort Burgwin. This was the first step in what later became a major effort to develop proper dormitory and kitchen/dining facilities at the Research Center.

New Wing on the Rounds Building and Problems with Investments

Two major developments occurred after the 1969 meeting of the Board. In the fall of 1969 I received an award from the NSF to complete the laboratory and office wing in the Rounds Building. The grant was supplemented by funds already pledged by Dwight Rounds. A few weeks later, plans were drawn, a contractor was hired, and work began on the building. It was completed in June 1970. This, and the geology dormitory, fulfilled the two initial requirements that had to be met by SMU according to the merger agreement.

The second major development I reported at the 1969 meeting of the Board was not so pleasant. The treasurer of the Rounds Foundation, at the suggestion of the investment officer of SMU, had invested all of the cash assets of the Fort Burgwin Research Center Endowment Fund in Texas Consumers Finance Corporation in Fort Worth, Texas. Seven months later, the corporation filed for bankruptcy. The court-approved repayment plan allowed Fort Burgwin to recover only 56 percent of the amount invested—and that only over a period of years, to end in 1978. This was a devastating blow to the development plans for the Research Center, and even now it is hard for me to understand why greater fiscal responsibility was not taken in the investment of those funds. In the near term, the loss was borne by Fort Burgwin, but ultimately SMU had to assume an even greater burden for the operation and maintenance of Fort Burgwin than would otherwise have been necessary.

In a Board report memorandum dated February 20, 1970, I included a detailed financial statement for the 1969–70 fiscal year that showed an estimated surplus of a few thousand dollars. This was the first time that the income of the Center had exceeded expenditures by more than a few hundred dollars. The surplus came about because the university had shifted my summer salary to the budget of the Anthropology Department, where I had been chairman since the department had been established in 1967. I noted that the reduction in expenditures would not continue, however, because the tentative budget for the fiscal year of July 1, 1970, through June 30, 1971, showed an estimated surplus of only a few hundred dollars.

After the merger in mid-1968, I had begun to think that I should resign from the Fort Burgwin Research Center Board of Trustees. My decision to do so was strongly influenced by my concern that there might be a conflict of interest with my position as the Center's Director, for which I reported to Albritton, who was also on the Board. Other vacancies on the Board occurred when Erwin, Mitchell, and Reed also resigned when I left the Board. At its 1970 meeting, George Lavender became President of the Board and Dwight Rounds became Chairman. The other remaining members on the Board were Albritton, Brandenburg, Sears, and Vickery. Six new members were elected to the Board at this time: Jack Boyer, Director of the Kit Carson Museum, in Taos; William B. Heroy, President and a major benefactor of the Institute for the Study of Earth and Man at SMU; Patrick James Kirby, a California attorney with a residence near Taos; William M. Pearce, an old friend of mine when we were both at Texas Tech and President of Texas Wesleyan University, in Fort Worth; Ina MacNaughton, widow of Lewis MacNaughton, and Marian Meyers, who returned to the Board as Secretary. One of the more important and, in my opinion, unfortunate actions taken at the annual meeting of the Board held on June 20, 1970, was to delete from the bylaws the term limitations for Board members and to extend the terms of the current members for the life of the corporation.

My report to the Board at this meeting included a revised financial statement for the 1969–70 fiscal year that showed more income than had been anticipated, due to a larger-than-expected distribution from the Fort Burgwin Research Center Endowment Fund, with a carryover of several thousand dollars. At the same meeting I urged the Board to authorize me to hire a resident manager to oversee routine chores in my absence. The Board agreed. I then prepared a revised budget for the 1970–71 fiscal year, with estimated income and expenditures and with a much smaller surplus. To fill the resident manager position, I employed someone whom I did not know but who came highly recommended. He proved to be unreliable, and I let him go a few months later. He was not replaced. I decided to keep on as before, without a resident manager.

In this same 1970 meeting, the Board also recognized Stephen Borhegyi's contributions in the installation of the museum exhibits in the west wing of the Rounds Building. The Board designated that wing of the building the Stephen Borhegyi Hall. The Board also inspected and accepted the new anthropology laboratory facilities.

Finally, I distributed copies of a preliminary plan developed by Louis Walker, the architect I had employed to prepare a plan for student housing and dining facilities. The proposed development would occur in four stages: (1) construct a dormitory for one hundred students and a sewage treatment plant; (2) build a combination dining and meeting facility; (3) build a second dormitory for another one hundred students and additional faculty housing; and (4) build a "little theater" and a third dormitory for eighty students. The plan was clearly premature, and I offered it only as a working document, because I knew of no source for the money that would be required. I also reported that I anticipated receiving from the SMU Development Office a proposal for the development of a conference center at Fort Burgwin.

Six field schools were conducted at the Research Center during the summer of 1970, with a total student enrollment of 107, plus faculty and staff. This was the largest group ever to utilize the Center's facilities during a single season, and all of them were at the Research Center at the same time, in June and July. The acceptable dormitories could accommodate only sixty at any one time; the others had to stay in town or in tents.

We were obviously overextended. But even though this represented a great strain on the Center facilities and staff, the problem was limited to a six-week period. The pressure during the first half of the summer existed because university students traditionally are reluctant to attend training programs at any time other than during the first half of the summer. Although a new schedule needed to be devised, I had yet to develop a suitable use for the facility during the remainder of the summer. Meanwhile, we planned to develop a broader base of SMU academic support for the Research Center, both to enhance the scholarly activity at Fort Burgwin and to strengthen university sponsorship.

The largest training program during the summer of 1970 was a high-school group of twenty-nine students and a staff of six, led by Jack Zahniser. The group came during the last part of the summer, but even then there were too many people for the available dormitory space. They camped out in tents, although they ate with us and used our toilet facilities. It was an interesting group; they received no academic credit, but they worked hard studying archaeology and several other subjects, such as photography and the identification of wild plants.

The geology field school sponsored by the University of North Carolina and Georgia State University was another large group; it consisted of twenty-five graduate and undergraduate students led by Charles Wagg. In addition, there were two archaeology field schools: one from SMU, directed by James Sciscenti with twenty-two students; and the other from Wake Forest University, with nine students led by Ned Woodall. The two groups worked together excavating a room-block at Pot Creek Pueblo. There were also two other SMU-sponsored field schools: one in linguistics, with seven students led by George Trager; and the other in ethnology, directed by Ben Wallace, with seventeen students.

The field schools had, for the moment, solved the immediate financial problems of the Fort Burgwin Research Center. However, the crowded conditions of the dormitories told me that I had to find a better solution.

CHAPTER 3

A New Campus for Fort Burgwin

In the spring of 1970, Fred Hoster, Director of Special Projects in the Development Office at SMU, came by my office at SMU for a visit. This visit started a chain of events that would ultimately lead to one of the most important developments in the history of the Fort Burgwin Research Center. Hoster had heard about Fort Burgwin, and he wanted to know more about it. I offered to fly him out to the Center for the weekend, and he readily accepted. I had taken up flying a year earlier and had bought a Cessna 172 so that I could commute to Taos at least once a month (when I was not in Egypt) and keep track of what was going on.

Like almost everyone else, as soon as Hoster saw the Little Rio Grande Valley, he was enchanted by the place and immediately recognized it as an asset that could have enormous potential for the university. Over a long evening in Taos with enchiladas and beer, we talked about the problems I faced in operating the Center, the precarious financial situation, and my hopes for the future of Fort Burgwin. We discussed the inadequate dormitory and dining facilities and how the Center would never be self-supporting unless the facilities could somehow be upgraded and expanded significantly. I told him I hoped to find a way to operate for most of the year and also include more of the university in its programs. Among other things, we talked about involving the university alumni in retreats and educational programs. At the end of the evening, he offered to help me find the funds to build the dormitories and other facilities that were needed for the Center to become self-supporting and also a true western campus for SMU.

When Hoster returned to Dallas, he began to assemble data on summer conference and recreational facilities, such as the ones operated by the Denver YMCA at Estes Park and Snow Mountain in Colorado. Hoster and I then began to sketch out a plan that he would present to the Fort Burgwin Board and then to SMU's Board of Governors. I also arranged for him to meet Louis Walker, of Santa Fe. Walker was my choice as the architect to design any new buildings at the Research Center.

A special called meeting of the Fort Burgwin Board was held at the First State Bank in Taos on April 3, 1971. First on the agenda were several routine items, such as noting that we had only a few hundred dollars on hand to last until the end of May and that several building repairs would have to be done. George Lavender expressed his unhappiness over James Sciscenti's work as Assistant Director. I told Lavender that Sciscenti had already resigned as Assistant Director but would remain in charge of the archaeology field school during the coming summer. I never did find out what had happened between those two men. I guess I did not try, because I regarded Jim Sciscenti to be an excellent archaeologist and a good friend. And George Lavender was also a good friend.

Hoster then presented his plan, and it was bold. First, he stated that his office would recommend that funding be found to develop the facilities needed to support a broadly based, first-class academic program at Fort Burgwin. He then described the YMCA conference facilities in Colorado and noted that they yielded an annual profit of between $400,000 and $500,000 per year. He observed that the program he envisioned was much smaller than the YMCA's programs; the overall philosophies were the same, although his proposed program was more academically focused: it was to be a multiphase program with facilities for students, alumni, and other families, as well as a conference and convention center, all with year-round operational capability. Hoster's plan called for facilities adequate for 250 people. This would require a co-ed dormitory for 100 students, 25 two-and three-bedroom "mountain homes," dining and conference facilities, plus natural gas, water, and sewer services. The houses were to be built of adobe in five different designs.

Hoster also discussed how the mountain homes could be financed. His idea was to approach corporations and friends of SMU with a proposal that they make a substantial, tax-deductible gift to the university; in exchange, they would be given priority use of a house for one month each year and would pay rent at the going rate. He had made preliminary inquiries to several potential participants, and he thought that finding twenty-five donors was feasible. In addition, he planned to approach individuals and major foundations for grants to build the multipurpose dining and conference/auditorium facilities or to seek financing through a bank loan, using the land as collateral.

This was an impressive plan. The Fort Burgwin Trustees were generally favorable, but they were concerned that these new facilities not intrude into the historical setting of the existing facilities. Some trustees urged caution in depending too heavily on revenue projections from the operation of the proposed conference center. They pointed out that the income from a similar center in Wichita had been disappointing to investors. Also, the trustees had serious reservations about using the land as collateral for a bank loan. Nevertheless, the trustees endorsed the proposal. Jack Brandenburg, George Lavender, and Dwight Rounds contributed a total of $2,000 to finance the preliminary preparations needed for a major fund-raising effort. A few days later Hoster gave a report on his proposal to SMU's Board of Governors and received their approval for the proposed expansion of Fort Burgwin. He also arranged for several members of the SMU Board to visit Fort Burgwin around the middle of August.

A second special Fort Burgwin Board meeting was held less than two months later, on June 26, 1971, to discuss the summer program and to consider Hoster's development plan for Fort Burgwin. By this time Hoster, Walker, and I had developed more details on costs and also a development schedule. The three basic recommendations for the Fort Burgwin Board were (1) send an official letter to the SMU Board of Governors giving approval for the project; (2) appoint a Fort Burgwin Board Committee to work closely with the SMU Board on the project; and (3) use a portion of the land as collateral to secure the funds required to implement the first phase of the project.

The first two recommendations were generally accepted by the Board, but the last suggestion was not approved. The Board wanted first to get the pledges for the initial 25 homes and then, if necessary, consider encumbering the land to build the sewer and service utilities. The trustees then passed a motion approving phase 1 of the summary plan. They authorized the SMU Development Office to secure pledges for the construction of a minimum of 25 two- and three-bedroom "mountain homes" and to solicit other funds to construct a central sewage facility, build the necessary roads, and install the required utilities. Walker was retained to prepare a map showing the proposed locations of the buildings, roads, and other service facilities for submission to the Fort Burgwin Board for its approval. The Fort Burgwin Board also recognized the need for additional facilities to house the students who attended the various field schools and other classes at the Research Center, and they viewed the proposed conference center as a likely source of significant financial support for Fort Burgwin. But they wanted to move with caution.

The need for additional dormitory and dining facilities was indicated by the activities at the Center during the summer of 1971. In the first half of the summer there were seven field schools in residence. The SMU archaeology field school, under my general direction, had seventeen students; the ethnology-linguistics field school, under George Trager, had sixteen students; the Wake Forest University field school, led by Ned Woodall, had thirteen students; and the geology field school, sponsored by the University of North Carolina and Georgia State University, had thirty-one students. With faculty supervisors and their families, the kitchen fed eighty-five people every day with two shifts at each meal. All of the field schools were finished by the middle of July, and in the second half of the summer there were only two classes. One of these was a high school group with thirty-five students led by Jack Zahniser; the other was an SMU-sponsored writers' workshop, also with thirty-five students, taught by Marshall Terry, of the Department of English at SMU. The tight financial situation was exacerbated by kitchen improvements required by the New Mexico Health Department and by the emergency replacement of a septic tank. Somehow, however, the expenditures did not exceed income. At the end of the fiscal year, there was a balance of a few hundred dollars. Perhaps at this point it is appropriate to note that I did not know it was possible to have a budget deficit; I thought that I would have to make up any overrun out of my own pocket!

At about this time, Claude Albritton, aware of the intense pressure on the available faculty and student facilities, became concerned that Marian Meyers, Secretary of the Fort Burgwin Board, might begin to think she had lifetime tenure in the commander's house at the fort, where she had lived since 1965. He requested that I ask her to give up the residence. She was understandably very upset with this news but nevertheless agreed to move as soon as possible. She was particularly unhappy with me because she felt that I should have protected her interests better, and in retrospect, she was probably correct. I suspect, however, that the result for her would have been the same.

For two years we had been using a part-time custodial staff for the summer months, with only Meyers in residence to protect the property durng the other nine months of the year. This was not safe for Meyers or adequate for the Research Center. So despite our limited budget, in late August I arranged for Tito Archuleta, a longtime employee at the now-closed Pot Creek sawmill, to become our full-time custodian. He and his wife, Florida (our cook since 1958), closed their house in Talpa and moved into the two-bedroom apartment at the west end of the fort compound. Except for the summers of 1971 through 1984, when they returned to their Talpa home because of the demand for housing at the fort, Tito and Florida remained at Fort Burgwin until 1993, when they both retired.

Clements Becomes Involved

On August 14, 1971, five members of the SMU Board of Governors flew in from Dallas to spend the day at Fort Burgwin. The Dallas group included the Board Chairman William P. Clements Jr. (Figure 24), Eugene McDermott, Robert Ritchie, C. A. Tatum, and Floyd James. In addition, James E. Brooks and Keith Baker, two senior members of the SMU faculty, and Fred Hoster came to the Center. The purpose of this meeting was to view the facilities at the

Figure 24.

William and Rita Clements.

Photo by Hillsman Jackson. Photo courtesy of Southen Methodist University photo archives.

fort and to discuss the new development plans with the Fort Burgwin Board. At a joint meeting, the two groups considered the program of the Research Center and discussed the need for the new facilities. The Fort Burgwin Board then reviewed the merger agreement with SMU and determined that by completing the anthropology laboratory and by constructing the dormitory for forty students, the university had fulfilled the initial terms of the merger. They then authorized the transfer of the remaining thirty-six acres of the campus proper to the university. The meeting was adjourned, and the group took a brief tour of the Research Center, including a visit to the archaeological excavations of Zahniser's high-school group at Pot Creek Pueblo. This was followed by a few margaritas and a steak lunch cooked over the outdoor grill in the main compound. After the lunch, the SMU group departed for Dallas. It had been a very successful meeting.

At my request, and after several years of negotiation, in January 1972 the Rounds family agreed to sell me four acres of land lying along the Little Rio Grande and adjoining the southern boundary of the fort property. I arranged for Walker to draw up preliminary plans for the house I wanted to build there, and in May 1972 my son Mike put up a fence. I bought and stored the *vigas* needed for the roof and flagstone for the floor. I got a well permit but held off on drilling the well until I had saved the money it would cost.

That winter I had a long and very demanding field season in Ethiopia and Egypt, lasting from early January until almost the end of April 1972, and when I returned to Dallas, I moved quickly to arrange for the coming summer activities at Fort Burgwin. I learned that Walker had made significant progress with the preliminary plans for the new facilities at Fort Burgwin. There was a problem, however. In April, Clements told me that he was concerned about the lack of zoning restrictions on the two properties adjoining Fort Burgwin on the south: the seventeen acres owned by Meyers; and the seventy-six acres owned by the Rounds Trust (from which I had purchased four acres). Clements added that SMU would not proceed with our development plans until that problem was resolved.

On May 29, 1972, I sent a progress report to the Fort Burgwin Board. I reported that SMU's development plan had been placed on hold because of the delay in negotiations concerning land adjacent to the proposed development area and because of the desire of the university to safeguard its investment. I noted, however, that other negotiations seemed to be proceeding satisfactorily. The SMU Board of Governors had authorized Clements to negotiate the purchase of one of the parcels of land. If this was accomplished, I thought that subsequent parts of the plan would move promptly. I also reported on a potentially dangerous fire in the sawdust in the old millpond and noted that I expected heavy use of the facilities over the coming summer, with four field school projects and the writers' workshop already scheduled.

Problems with the Fort Burgwin Board

The next meeting of the Fort Burgwin Board, on June 12, 1972, was difficult. I began by discussing the need for repairs to the roofs on the Rounds Building and the staff apartment buildings. I also noted that we had six manuscripts ready to be published, and I reported on the anticipated field schools and other research activities planned for the coming summer. I then followed up on my May 29, 1972, report to the Board regarding Clements's concerns about the lands adjoining the fort. I related a conversation that I had had with Clements in late April, when he had first informed me of his concern about the lack of zoning restrictions on the two properties in private ownership to the south of Fort Burgwin. Clements was concerned that someone might buy that land and put in a trailer park, a gasoline station, or some other undesirable development that would adversely affect the plans for Fort Burgwin. He told me that unless his concerns were resolved, SMU would not put any money into the proposed development project.

This discussion brought an immediate protest from Meyers, who owned one of the parcels of land. She was offended that these conversations had taken place without her knowledge. She stated that under no circumstances would she agree to restrict or sell her property. A resolution was then passed requesting that SMU furnish the Fort Burgwin Board with information concerning the specific development plans that the university had adopted for the property held in its name, or in trust for Fort Burgwin, and for the land adjacent to Fort Burgwin. At the time, I did not understand the basis for Meyers's anger. I had informed her of Clements's concern, and I felt that all she needed to say was that she was capable of looking after the interests of her land and Fort Burgwin and then let the issue drop. My mistake was in not discussing Clements's concerns privately with the other Board members from Taos prior to the June meeting. It was an unfortunate failure of communication on my part.

Later in the meeting, Lavender obtained a resolution authorizing him, on behalf of the Fort Burgwin Board, to request an annual statement from the Rounds Foundation providing full information on the status of the Fort Burgwin Endowment Fund and annual income. This raised my concerns even higher, because this motion and the previous discussion indicated a developing lack of trust between the Fort Burgwin Board and SMU. I was caught by surprise, but I suspected that Meyers had convinced Lavender and perhaps others that she had been treated unfairly by SMU in regard to the commander's house. My lapse in communication had obviously contributed to the uncomfortable situation. In any event, Meyers had become an enemy, and from this point on, she used every opportunity to be difficult.

At this meeting, I also told the Fort Burgwin Board that after my conversation with Clements, I had gone to Wichita to see if the Rounds family would sell its remaining land to SMU. The family had seemed interested, and I had passed the word on to Clements. At the meeting of the SMU Board of Governors in mid-May, Clements had obtained authorization to purchase the land, if possible. After taking a trip to Wichita, Clements had called and told me that he had bought the seventy-six acres of land from the Rounds family in the name of SMU.

The Fort Burgwin Board met again on August 5, 1972. Among those present were Clements, Brooks, and Bill Heroy Jr., Treasurer and Vice President for Finance at SMU. The minutes show that I gave a report on the activities at the Research Center and also presented a detailed budget and financial report dated July 24, 1972. The report was for the period from July 1, 1971, to May

31, 1972 (SMU had changed the end of its fiscal year to May 31). I also gave the trustees a budget of expenditures for the 1972–73 fiscal year. In stark contrast to Secretary Meyers's minutes for every previous Board meeting, her minutes for this meeting are very limited and give none of the details of my reports.

The minutes also do not indicate that Clements and I showed the Board the site plans for locations of the dormitories, the dining/meeting hall, and the service roads. By this time we had decided to build ten small dormitories, each with room for ten students (later modified to eight units, two being doubles with room for twenty students). The preliminary plans that we showed the Board indicated that each unit had a sleeping area, a large living room with a fireplace, and a generous bathroom. Meyers's diluted minutes did not include two other items that are of particular interest in light of later developments: the first was that Clements and I were meeting with the architect in two days to authorize construction plans for the dining facility and the dormitories to house one hundred students; and the second was that SMU had purchased the seventy-six acres from the Rounds estate. This purchase had been made possible by a contribution from Clements.

On October 12, 1972, Clements invited Brooks, Heroy, Robert Ritchie, Edgar F. Hoffman (an SMU Building and Grounds staff member), and me to go with him in his company plane to Taos so that we could look over the Fort Burgwin campus again and discuss my plans for new facilities. I told him about Hoster's proposal, which I weakly supported. He responded by telling me that he was not very impressed with the idea of a conference center. He thought it would ruin the rural atmosphere of the Little Rio Grande Valley—the atmosphere that made the fort so attractive. Then he asked me what I really wanted and needed to make a proper campus for SMU's programs at the Center. I did not disagree with him about the possible impact of Hoster's plans on the environment, possibly because subconsciously I was not too sure I wanted to manage a conference center. In any case, I told Clements I wanted dormitory facilities for one hundred students, a dining/meeting facility for the same number, and the roads and other services for those facilities. I also told him I wanted these new facilities to be hidden in the woods, with a series of small units, rather than one or two large buildings. Clements did not respond, but I could tell from his expression that this was more in line with his ideas.

As we walked over the area, Clements described to me his vision for the development of Fort Burgwin. He wanted to invite wealthy friends of SMU to build homes here—not the modest mountain homes that Hoster and I had proposed but, rather, large houses. He felt that this would develop into an important financial commitment that would ensure the continued growth of Fort Burgwin. There was no room in this vision for the proposed conference center. I reasoned that it could be built later if SMU at some point decided that the university needed a conference center on the campus. As we were walking back to the cars, Clements told me that he would provide the funds needed to build the dormitories and the dining facility that I had described to him, as well as the service facilities they would require.

But he had one condition. While we were walking together away from the others, Clements told me that before he would give the money I wanted for the new facilities, I would have to sell to SMU, at my cost, the four acres of land that I had bought several months earlier from the Rounds family. I understood his concern, because when I had bought the land, it was at the southern edge of the fort property. Now, with his recent purchase of the seventy-six acres from the Rounds family, my property was near the center of the land owned by the fort. I offered to make a swap for four acres somewhere out of the way, near the edge of the property. He would not agree. He said he did not want any faculty to own houses at Fort Burgwin. I had a choice: new facilities that I very much wanted and no house site for me, or no new facilities. We left for Dallas that afternoon, but we had engine trouble on Clements's new plane and landed in Lubbock. Before we took a commercial flight on to Dallas, Clements and I again discussed my land. I assured him that I would sell my land to the university when we returned to Dallas. Later that week, as promised, I sold my land to SMU.

Although I find it understandable why Clements put such pressure on me to sell my land to the university, I did not like his ultimatum. The construction plans for my house had already been drawn, a fence had been erected, and the *vigas* to support the roof had been cut and peeled. I had planned to build the house during the coming summer. Even though I was sympathetic with Clements when he insisted that I sell those four acres to SMU, I did not understand why a swap for the same amount of land somewhere else, somewhere out of the way, would not have been acceptable. He refused to even consider such a swap and instead told me that I could construct my home anywhere I liked on the Fort Burgwin property now owned by SMU. I was naive enough at that time to think this was a reasonable arrangement, and in a visit to the fort later that summer, we went together to pick out a fine site for my house at the southern end of the land acquired from the Rounds estate. We also selected another site where he would build a house for himself. Later, after the dormitories were built in the summer of 1973, it became clear to me that I had not understood the implications of the agreement I had made with Clements. When I went to my local bank in Taos, I learned that because I would not own the land, no one would give me financing to build my home.

My pride would not permit me to tell Clements that I could not afford to build a house on someone else's property, and so I never even discussed this with him. We continued to be good friends. A few years later he arranged for President Ronald Reagan to appoint me to the Secretary of Interior's National Park Service Advisory Board. Looking back, I guess it is understandable why I did not resist Clements's pressure on me to sell my land. He was, after all, the chairman of SMU's Board of Governors, and I very much wanted those facilities and what they would do for the Fort Burgwin Research Center. In time, however, and especially after I was no longer connected with the Center, I came to resent the price I had paid.

Completing the Museum Exhibits

The research activities conducted at the Research Center during the summer of 1972 included the SMU archaeological field school, with twenty students led by Joel Shiner, by then a professor at SMU; an SMU ethnology field school, with ten students directed by Joseph Aceves, of SMU; an SMU art workshop, with twenty students under William Jordan, from the SMU Meadows School of the Arts; and a geology field school, with twenty-three students led by Robert Butler, of the University of North Carolina, and Charles Wagg, of Georgia State University. In the second half of the summer there was another SMU-sponsored writers' workshop, with twenty students under the supervision of Marshall Terry.

Also in the summer of 1972, two volunteers, Herbert and Shirley Achor, contributed their time to complete Stephen Borhegyi's exhibits in the museum. They followed the plans developed earlier by Borhegyi and by Curry and Fran Holden. Herbert Achor was a commercial artist in Dallas, and Shirley Achor was a graduate student in anthropology at SMU. They did an excellent job of installing the exhibits.

Sometime after the beginning of the 1972–73 fiscal year, I learned that SMU had established a new budget structure for Fort Burgwin to reflect the diverse activities now under way. The budget was divided into three major categories: the administration and maintenance of the Center; the field schools and other educational activities; and the kitchen operations. This revised financial statement was first distributed to the Fort Burgwin Board in June 1973, after the end of that fiscal year. It disclosed that both the archaeology field school and the kitchen had exceeded their budgets. These extra expenditures were covered by funds in the administrative budget, but they indicated that I needed to keep tighter control over expenditures and income in every budget area.

Building the New Casitas

The summer of 1973 was an exceptionally busy one for me. By then, Clements was in Washington, D.C., as Deputy Secretary of Defense. Before he left, he had asked me to personally supervise the construction of the new facilities at Fort Burgwin. He told me that he liked what I had done in reconstructing the original buildings of the cantonment. There was no budget for the new facilities; no limit was placed on how much I could spend. Clements wanted a first-class job, and he said that I should use my best judgment without bothering to ask him about details. Of course, I did not believe that I was completely on my own, and when a decision had to be made as to whether to put the electric service above or below ground (the difference in cost was $25,000), I called Clements in D.C. and asked what he preferred. After he asked me what I preferred, I said, "below ground." He told me to always do what I thought best and that would be fine with him. That was the last time I called him until after the dormitories were finished.

Walker had designed the dormitories to be simple so that their construction would not exceed my experience and abilities (Figure 25). We decided that we would build the eight dormitories, which we called "casitas," during the summer because the construction plans for these were ready, whereas the final plans for the dining/meeting building would not be completed until later in the summer. Because I had to be back in Dallas by the end of August and, perhaps even more important, because the dining/meeting building would require complex electrical and ventilation systems that were far beyond my experience, it seemed appropriate for that building to be constructed by a professional contractor. In early May 1973, work began on grading the access roads to the eight new dormitories. Plumbing and electrical contractors were found with the help of Ed Hoffman, and arrangements were made for the delivery of ready-mix concrete for the foundations, floors, and bond beams when needed. At the same time roof *vigas*, flagstone, lumber for the roofs, insulation, nails, plaster, and stucco were purchased and stored in the old schoolhouse. I also bought several thousand adobe bricks and arranged to have the required number delivered adjacent to each building as soon as the foundations and floors were poured. Throughout this project, Tito Archuleta, the custodian and resident manager of the fort, assisted me. In late May, with Tito's advice, I hired sixty local laborers, paying 10 percent over the local going wage. Tito selected the workers and kept things going smoothly.

Work began with the digging of the foundations and the setting of the initial pipes for the plumbing and the conduits for the electrical service. We decided to do several of the foundations and floors as quickly as possible, then leave some

Figure 25.

Fred Wendorf and Louis Walker discussing plans for the new dormitories and dining hall.

Photographer unknown. Photo courtesy of Fred Wendorf.

workers to complete the rest of the foundations and assign most of the crew to constructing two of the casitas simultaneously (Figure 26). With Tito's guidance, the construction went forward without a hitch. We both worked alongside the workmen, laying adobes, setting the roof beams, and nailing the roof boards. A locally famous fireplace builder was hired to build the fireplaces in each of the living rooms. As soon as the walls were up, she would begin to build the fireplace, finishing each one before the ceiling deck was installed.

Figure 26.

Construction under way for a new casita at Fort Burgwin, 1973.

Photo by Fred Wendorf.

I planned that two of the dormitories would be finished and roofed at about the same time. This schedule worked very well; even before the roofs were placed, most of the men working on those two buildings had moved on to the next two buildings, where the concrete foundations and floors were already in place. They began by laying the adobe walls. Meanwhile a plaster and stucco crew would finish the interiors and exteriors of the two roofed structures, the doors and windows would be hung, and the plumbers and electricians would complete the installation of their fixtures. By mid-August we were finishing the last building. It took ten weeks to finish all of the casitas (Figure 27).

Labor Troubles at the Casitas

Of the activities during the dormitory construction, only one incident merits recording. Our crew was composed of local Hispanic Americans, all hard workers. One day in early July two young Anglos showed up and asked if I could put them to work. Tito was against it, but they seemed willing and strong, so I went ahead and hired them. Two days later I was having lunch at my house when Tito drove up hurriedly and rushed in to tell me the men had gone on strike for higher wages. I told him to go back and tell the men that I would be there in a few minutes. I brought my payroll records and checkbook with me, and when I arrived, the men were in an ugly mood. I gathered them all together and told them that I was sorry but that I had no authority to increase their wages. If they wanted to leave, I would pay them off now, as of noon that day. I urged them to think it over, adding that the wage I was paying was over the going rate, and I

Figure 27.

Completed casita, ready for student occupants.

Photo by Fred Wendorf.

asked them to come back the next day. I told them that anyone who showed up at seven the next morning would have his job back but that I would hire replacement workers for those who did not show up. As each man came forward I handed him his check, shook his hand, thanked him for the work he had done, and urged him to come back the next day.

After everyone had left, I was very dejected and worried about how I could finish the job. But I need not have been concerned because meanwhile, Florida, Tito's wife, had gotten on the telephone and was calling the wives, girlfriends, and/or mothers of every worker. When the men got home that evening (no doubt after stopping at the local bar and spending some of the money I had given them), I am sure they received an unfriendly reception. Tito was also busy; he got in touch with many others he knew who would like to work and told them about the situation: that there might be jobs the next morning at 7:00 a.m. The word spread, and the next morning when I drove up to the old schoolhouse, more than one hundred men were there. I did not know if there would be trouble, but when I saw the smiles on the faces of my crew, I stopped worrying and began calling the roll. Everyone was there except the two Anglos, so I told those who remained that I had only two vacancies. I asked who had been the first to arrive, a man held up his hand, and I hired him; then I asked who had arrived next, and I hired him. I told the others that I hoped I would not need any more men, but in case I did, I asked that they leave their names with Tito.

There were no other problems the rest of the summer. I later learned that the two Anglo boys had no sooner been hired than they had immediately started urging the men to go on strike, telling them that SMU was a rich school and should pay Dallas wages, not Taos wages. A few weeks after the "strike," the two boys showed up and asked for their jobs back, but I told them their jobs had been filled. I asked Tito to see that they were off our land.

More Problems with the Fort Burgwin Board

The Fort Burgwin Board held its next annual meeting on August 18, 1973. I had been busy building the new dormitories and had had no opportunity to prepare a financial statement or a written report on activities at the Research Center, but I did prepare a preliminary statement in which I anticipated that expenditures would increase in the next year because more janitorial services and utilities would be needed. The meeting minutes are strangely brief regarding activities and do not cover that part of the meeting. I know there was an SMU archaeological field school led by Joel Shiner, but I have no records of other groups or activities at the Center that summer. The minutes do note that I told the Board about the progress with the dormitories, the mess hall, the 100,000-gallon water-storage tank that had been installed on the hill southwest of the fort, the underground electrical system, and the road construction. I also reported that Jim Hester's report on Blackwater Draw had been published and that Ernestine Green's report on pithouse occupations in the Taos Valley was about to go to press. I also noted that the Research Center had purchased a new flatbed truck to help with the construction and that it would be available in future years for work around the campus.

Meyers then offered a motion that the Fort Burgwin Research Center Board dissolve immediately. In the following discussion, a series of complaints were expressed: I had failed to obtain approval of the Board before proceeding with the construction of the new dormitories (evidently there had been no formal motion of approval, although I thought I had their support when Clements and I met with them in August 1972); SMU had purchased land from the Rounds family without Board approval; and SMU had urged a risky investment of the Fort Burgwin Endowment Fund without the participation of the Board.

I responded that although I had perhaps erred in not seeking formal approval of the final construction plans, I thought Clements and I had fully consulted with them as to our intentions. I wondered in what way SMU could actually be more helpful to the functioning of the Board. I also stated that I valued their advice and support, that we had all struggled hard to get the fort to the stage where it now was, and that I thought they would be pleased at what had been accomplished. At this point Brandenburg offered a note of caution, observing that SMU would surely like to continue to have a few people interested in Fort Burgwin, at least until 1979 when the endowment property was to be transferred to SMU. After a few more comments by George Lavender,

Paul Sears suggested that the motion offered by Meyers be tabled until the next meeting. Meyers then submitted her resignation as Secretary-Treasurer; however, I (unwisely) urged her to reconsider because in the past, she had been very helpful to the fort and to me and because I highly valued her advice. She agreed not to make a final decision until the next meeting.

I saw that the time I had spent arranging for the new campus and supervising and actively participating in the construction of the new buildings and service facilities had adversely affected my communication with the Board. I was surprised when I realized that Meyers had used this period to develop sympathy for her and hostility toward SMU among the Board members (especially George Lavender) over the request that she vacate the commander's house. This acrimony had jeopardized the program at the Research Center just as we were about to achieve some of our long-term goals. As it turned out, Meyers stayed on the board, finally retiring several years after I had left the Fort Burgwin Research Center. Still later, she moved to California.

Wetherington Comes to Help

I realized that Fort Burgwin had grown beyond what I could manage on a part-time basis without some help, and so I turned to my old friend and colleague Ronald Wetherington for assistance. Wetherington had great affection for the Research Center; he had first come to the fort as a graduate student and had been my assistant in the excavation of Pot Creek Pueblo. He had written his Ph.D. dissertation on his work at Pot Creek, and he and I had come to SMU at the same time. I asked Wetherington to be Associate Director; in this position, he would be responsible for the routine management of the fort and would help me develop an academic program that would involve a broad spectrum of interests at SMU and in the Taos community. Privately, I thought that he might succeed me should I step down as Director, an action that I was considering.

In late September, a contract was let for the construction of the dining/

meeting facility. The building was to be finished and ready for use before the students arrived in the following June. It was to have a fully modern kitchen and seating for more than one hundred diners.

In March 1974, I sent the Board a financial report that showed, for the first time in my tenure as Director, a projected and significant deficit. The record does not show the Board's reaction, but I recall that Brooks, who was by then Provost of SMU, told me that I should not worry, that he could accept a deficit of that size. This was the first time I knew that I could have an explainable budget deficit. During the years when the Center had been independent, I could not have a deficit because there was no extra money available to cover any shortfall. I had just continued to assume that a budget was a firm commitment for expenditures that could not be exceeded.

On July 27, 1974, the eight new dormitories and the spacious new dining hall were formally dedicated by Deputy Secretary of Defense William P. Clements at a ceremony before 150 guests including Senator John Tower, the SMU Board of Governors, and the Fort Burgwin Research Center Board of Trustees. As part of the ceremony, Clements received the honorary degree of Doctor of Humane Letters from SMU. In his acceptance speech, Clements expressed his love of the land and his belief that all who were students and all who taught at Fort Burgwin would strengthen our nation because of the values they had received here. A news story about the event noted: "Mr. Clements' concern with the sylvan setting of the campus, located in the Rocky Mountains of northern New Mexico, eight miles southeast of Taos, was evident in the new structures. The buildings were carefully placed among the foothills; none is visible from the highway, and each is secluded within the campus area so not to offend the natural beauty of the landscape. Each adobe *casita* houses ten students and—true to Southwestern tradition—each has its own fireplace with built-in *bancos* (seats). The student center/dining hall complex, with its sweeping lines, soaring windows, and curved walls dominating the architecture, has been described as 'Frank Lloyd Wright in Adobe.'"

In the process of building the casitas, however, I had made two very serious mistakes. The first was that I had built dormitories in which there was one large bedroom with bunk beds, a large toilet/shower area, and a living room. At that time, these were fine accommodations for unmarried students. But I had completely blocked out Hoster's plans for educational programs for adults, alumni colleges, and the like at Fort Burgwin. This mistake significantly limited the use of the Center by families and married students.

The other mistake was almost as serious. I accepted the recommendation of the architect, Walker, to use electrical service for heating in the dormitories and for cooking in the dining hall. Electrical heating is very expensive, and the electric bill today represents a significant portion of the cost of operating Fort Burgwin. At the time the casitas were built, I could have arranged for natural gas to be brought to the fort at very little cost, but doing so now would be prohibitive. I did negotiate a very favorable rate with the Taos manager of the Kit Carson Electric Cooperative, the local electric utility, but that agreement lasted only as long as I was Director. I suppose I assumed that accepting an agreement with a handshake was enough to make it last forever. I should have known that when dealing with a corporation, one needs a signed written agreement. Electricity is very expensive in the Taos area, and that mistake has cost SMU dearly over the years.

The problem of heating the student dormitories also led to an interesting—and perhaps humorous—incident involving some of the students in two of the dormitories. It was early June 1974 and the first morning of classes. I went around to check on things in the new dormitories. I found the doors and windows open and the heaters on full-blast in both of the casitas where the women students were living. I turned off the heaters and closed the doors and windows, and later that afternoon I met with the students, told them that heating was very expensive, and asked them to please turn off the heaters if they had the doors and windows open. They promised to do so, but the next morning when I checked again, the doors and windows were open and the heaters were on. So we had another meeting, and another promise was made to turn off the heaters. Then on the third morning, I found the same situation; this time I did not say anything but simply went to the circuit boxes and removed the circuit breakers for the heaters in both of these casitas.

Now, for the previous eighteen years, the students in the various field schools had been living in logging shacks without any heat at all, and had evidently fared very well, so I was not worried. That night, however, it snowed. Among the students in one of those dorms was the daughter of my boss, Claude Albritton. Early the next morning a delegation of young women, led by Miss Albritton, descended on my house to demand that I do something about the heat in their casitas. We had a serious discussion about electric heaters and open windows, and I told them about previous generations of students who had never had any heat at all. This time they made a solemn promise that if I would reconnect the heaters, they would never leave the doors and windows open. I did so, and there was no more trouble for the rest of the summer. But when I saw Albritton a couple of months later, he said to me, "I understand you had some problem with heat in the dormitories." I replied, "Yes, but not anymore." With that he smiled, and we talked about other things.

Problems with the Board Are Over

The next annual meeting of the Fort Burgwin Board occurred on August 10, 1974. The hostile mood of the previous meeting had completely disappeared. Over the intervening months, the members of the Board had come to accept that their role was not supervisory but rather was advisory and that SMU very much desired their support and advice. The meeting began with Brooks expressing SMU's gratitude for the Board members' many years of service, which had made the new facilities possible. He closed by saying that SMU needed the advice of this Board and wanted the members to continue. Sears then made a motion to approve all of the physical facilities at the fort, with a special thanks to me for my role in that development. The motion was approved unanimously. This was followed by a discussion of the Board's advisory role to the university, and then a decision was made that the Board should return to rotating memberships with staggered terms of three years each. Lots were drawn to implement the staggered terms immediately.

At this point I introduced Wetherington, who reviewed the academic programs that had occurred during the summer. Together, Wetherington and I had decided to broaden the course offerings beyond the traditional field schools, and in his written report, he noted that there had been a total of 130 students in residence during the two summer terms (76 in the first term and 54 in the second), with a total of twenty courses offered: eight courses in the natural sciences and mathematics, six in social sciences, and six in the humanities. Student enrollment, however, was disappointing. The 110 course enrollments were not sufficient for the twelve faculty in residence. It is my understanding that low course enrollment remains a problem even today; no one has yet found the magic formula to induce more students to attend the classes offered at the Center during the last half of the summer. Wetherington then told the Board about the Colloquium Series that he had organized. Eight public lectures, one each week, were delivered beginning in early June, with an average attendance of sixty-five people at each lecture.

Near the end of the meeting Lavender brought up the resignation of Meyers as Secretary-Treasurer. Her resignation was unanimously approved, with gratitude for her years of service. She did not, however, resign from the Board. After further discussion, the Board decided to eliminate the office of Treasurer, and Judith Wetherington, Ron's wife, was appointed Secretary.

The only records I could find relating to the fiscal year 1974–75 are the minutes of the Fort Burgwin Board of Trustees annual meeting that occurred on August 9, 1975. According to these minutes, my report to the Board included a three-page financial statement showing a large deficit in operations and maintenance (of which salaries were almost half), in the academic budget, and in the kitchen. This was clearly unacceptable to me and, I am sure, to SMU, although I cannot recall any comment on the matter by Provost Brooks.

Funds from the endowment were kept in a separate account and showed a balance. The expenditures from the endowment fund included four fellowships, the reprinting of *Taos Adobes,* and the publication of *Blackwater Locality Number 1,* by Jim Hester, and *Pithouse Villages near Taos,* by Ernestine Green.

I then reported that the Reverend Robert Kennaugh, of Taos and Corsicana, Texas, was in the process of donating a large collection of Navajo and Zuni silver to Fort Burgwin.

Wetherington next handed out a two-page report on activities at the Research

Figure 28.
Edith and Peter O'Donnell.

Photographer unknown. Photo courtesy of Edith O'Donnell.

Center during the summer of 1975. He noted that twenty-nine courses had been offered, fourteen in the first term and fifteen in the second. There were 170 enrollments (up from 110 in the previous summer): 63 in the biological sciences, 65 in the social sciences, and 42 in the humanities. Although improved, student enrollment was still too low for a faculty of nineteen. Wetherington noted that in addition to the usual SMU-sponsored archaeology and ethnology field schools, four non-SMU groups were utilizing the Research Center: the University of North Carolina and the University of Texas geology field schools, a group from Birmingham Southern University, and a joint interdisciplinary program by Portland State University and the Western Natural History Institute. He also reported that the Colloquium Series had been expanded to include a full schedule of films as well as lectures and that two informal courses had been offered to the community during the summer. Wetherington clearly was responding to my request that he increase the offerings by Fort Burgwin, both in academic courses and in his Taos outreach programs. Later that summer, Peter and Edith O'Donnell (Figure 28) made a gift to the Fort Burgwin Research Center to endow the Colloquium Series in archaeology as a wedding present for Bill and Rita Clements.

I Decide to Resign as Director

Under the rules adopted the previous year, the terms of four members of the Board expired at this meeting: Claude Albritton, Patrick James Kirby, Ina MacNaughton, and Paul Sears. Albritton and Kirby had offered their resignations, but MacNaughton and Sears were reelected for three-year terms. Tenny Carter, of Taos, was elected to fill one of the vacancies.

At that point I informed the Board that I would resign as Director effective at the end of March 1976. I added that I hoped Ron Wetherington would succeed me but that I would urge Brooks to discuss the appointment with the Board before any action was taken. My decision to resign was motivated by a number of factors. Years ago I had become an archaeologist because I wanted to do archaeology; I enjoyed research, and I had developed a strong interest in North African prehistory. With the new facilities and academic programs, the directorship of the Fort Burgwin Research Center had become a major responsibility, and if I performed the job properly, I would have little time available for my research. My concern was not just the two or three months I would be in the field in Africa; I needed time to write and publish the results of that research if I was ever to become a successful scholar. I knew that I was trying to do too many things and that both my research and my administrative duties were suffering as a consequence.

Two friends of mine, Owen Henderson and Russ Morrison, both benefactors of SMU, had just established an endowed chair for me; they had asked that I concentrate on research and relinquish all administrative duties, including the chairmanship of the Department of Anthropology and the directorship of the Fort Burgwin Research Center. Had I not already felt that I had achieved most of what I had hoped to accomplish at the Center, I might have been able to persuade them to let me stay with Fort Burgwin, but I felt their request was probably best for me. I also thought that the Center would be in very capable hands with Wetherington. Wetherington succeeded me in April 1976, and he quickly introduced a series of new programs that were highly successful. SMU student participation increased, he received outside (NSF) funding to support a new innovative research and training program, and he successfully reached out to the Taos community with his popular Colloquium Series. These new activities were expensive, however. Even before I left, expenditures had risen sharply, particularly in the academic area. Because of the resulting budget deficit and perhaps other reasons unknown to me, Wetherington lost the confidence of Brooks after eighteen months. He was removed as Director in September 1977. Thomas E. Williams, a professor of geology at SMU, was appointed as the next director.

Even though I knew it was time for me to move on in March 1976, I questioned the wisdom of my decision in one very important way. I was concerned that Clements might feel I had let him down. He had placed a lot of trust in me when he had let me build the new dormitories, and he might be justified in feeling that I should stay as Director until the program we had discussed was fully established. Regardless, I needed to simplify my life and focus on the archaeology that I enjoyed so much. Besides, I felt that twenty years was enough; I had done my share of "institution building," and it was time for others to take over. Except for one or two brief periods when I served on Fort Burgwin committees and a year when I served as a member of the Board, I had little to do with Fort Burgwin after April 1976.

CHAPTER 4

A Time of Transition

JAMES E. BROOKS

MY FIRST CONTACT WITH FORT BURGWIN CAME DURING THE SUMMER of 1964, just before Fred Wendorf joined the SMU faculty. Early that summer, Wendorf was in Dallas to conclude his employment arrangements with SMU and to find a house for him and his family. At that time he was living at Fort Burgwin with several of his archaeological group with whom he had been associated on the Nubian project (and who would join him in the newly created archaeology group at SMU). During that visit Claude Albritton, then Dean of the Graduate School at SMU, arranged a luncheon to introduce Wendorf to a handful of his colleagues-to-be. The luncheon was held in the faculty dining room in Lawyer's Inn. As Chair of the Department of Geological Sciences, I was included in the group. The conversation turned immediately to Fort Burgwin and Fred's hopes for it to become a research center for the field sciences—specifically archaeology, geology, and probably, field biology. Based on that conversation, I immediately became interested in Fort Burgwin as a possible location for an ongoing geology summer field school that would be associated with relevant research programs centered in, but not limited to, the northern Rio Grande Valley. The model I had in mind was the Red Lodge–Bighorn Basin Field Studies Center in southern Montana and northern Wyoming, in which Princeton University was a principal participant. I decided to visit Fort Burgwin as soon as possible to explore the feasibility of this idea.

James E. Brooks is Professor Emeritus (Geology) and Provost Emeritus at Southern Methodist University.

It should be noted parenthetically that Albritton, himself a geologist, had a longstanding interest in archaeology, going back at least to his days in graduate school at Harvard. There he had been greatly influenced by courses and fieldwork with Kirk Bryan, a legendary figure in the application of geology and geomorphology to the interpretation of archaeological sites. In addition, Albritton was deeply committed to the concept of building universities by building or finding and importing centers of academic strength. Clearly he saw in the Wendorf group such an opportunity. Fort Burgwin came with the group to SMU as a bonus—or perhaps, as President Willis Tate may have thought on a few days, as a "New Mexico Alligator Farm."

A few weeks after the luncheon meeting with Wendorf, my family and I were on our way to Colorado for vacation. We detoured by Fort Burgwin to see the location firsthand. We were immediately captivated by the property and the ambience of northern New Mexico. That fall, the SMU Department of Geological Sciences began plans to offer a summer field course at Fort Burgwin in the following summer. The course was developed and led by Professor Eugene Herrin. That course was offered for a number of years, for a while jointly with the University of North Carolina and later by the University of North Carolina alone, under the leadership of David Dunn, an SMU geology alumnus (B.S. and M.S.) and a faculty member at North Carolina. Herrin, who had growing commitments to the U.S. government (the Department of Defense), found it increasingly difficult to block out six weeks away from Dallas, and he withdrew from the course at Burgwin. During this time my interest in the fort and its programs continued, but the direct participation by the Department of Geological Sciences did not resume until several years later.

During the early years Fort Burgwin had, of course, been a separately incorporated entity under the laws of the state of New Mexico and had its own Board of Directors. All of this is described in detail by Wendorf in the previous three chapters. The plan to convey Fort Burgwin to SMU over a twenty-one-year period beginning in 1968 is described in detail by Wendorf, as is the changing makeup and function of the Fort Burgwin Board. If the fort had been able to achieve the financial independence that would have enabled it to carry out the programs that Ralph Rounds and Wendorf had envisioned, it is doubtful that it would have come to SMU. As it was, the growing association with SMU gave the fort the organizational and financial stability that was needed for it to succeed, and the fort gave the university a distinctive element that, properly developed, could help distinguish SMU as an important private university.

In 1969 I became Associate Provost and Dean of Faculties of Humanities and Sciences at SMU, assuming overall coordinating and administrative responsibilities for the graduate and undergraduate programs in humanities and sciences and for University College, the liberal arts core educational program of the university. My new responsibilities also included Fort Burgwin. Shortly after my appointment, Wendorf paid me a visit to "bring me up to speed" on the fort. While in my office, he said, "And, by the way, you may not know that part of the agreement which the university signed with the Fort Burgwin Board was that the university would put a minimum of $10,000 a year into the development of the fort, and I want to be sure that at least that amount is in your budget!" At that time, $10,000 was a significantly large amount of money. But for the fort to eventually pass fully to SMU, this condition had to be met, and it was! From that point until 1984, I played an increasingly more active role in the fort—its programs, its growth, and its administration.

Although I had no "official" position in relation to the Fort Burgwin Board in those days, I made a point to attend all of its meetings. During the 1960s and 1970s, the Board functioned, quite appropriately, largely independently of SMU. As a result, the makeup of the Board, both those members representing SMU and those members from Taos, was quite important. It was my judgment that although Wendorf was a strong presence, respected by all, the Taos members of the Board needed to begin to feel some growing acquaintance with the SMU administration. During this time Albritton rotated off the Fort Burgwin Board, which was another reason for me to become more active.

I wanted to begin to encourage the development of appropriate academic programs for Fort Burgwin. In those years Marshall Terry was building a writing program in the SMU Department of English. The first D. H. Lawrence Conference was held in Taos (or, more accurately, at the D. H. Lawrence

Ranch north of Taos) in October 1970. Terry was interested in participating, as was also Bryce Morrison, a young member of the English Department faculty. The three of us attended the conference. In addition to seeing and hearing from some of the colorful characters who had been associated with Lawrence, Terry had an opportunity to become acquainted with Fort Burgwin. The next summer and for a number of summers thereafter, Terry and his writing associates at SMU and in the Southwest conducted a very successful writing workshop at Fort Burgwin, adding an appropriate dimension to the program possibilities for the fort.

The Beginning of Transition

By 1971, through the efforts of a number of us, certainly including Wendorf, knowledge of Fort Burgwin and its potential was spreading. Of particular importance in this achievement was William P. Clements Jr., the chairman of the SMU Board of Governors (the Executive Committee of the SMU Board of Trustees). Clements, a southwestern history buff, had made at least one private visit to Taos to "scope out" this property that SMU was in the process of acquiring. As has happened to many, he was captivated by Taos and its environs and, in this case, the quiet valley in which Fort Burgwin sits. Clements was convinced that this could become a real university asset. On May 24, 1971, he convened a meeting about Fort Burgwin and its potential development. Present were Wendorf, Keith Baker (Vice President for Development), Larry TerMolen (Director of Development), Fred Hoster (TerMolen's assistant), and me. The subject was how best to widen the base of support for the fort among the SMU Board of Governors and, ultimately, to a wider community.

Following this meeting, in rapid succession, I had meetings with Bill Wright from SMU's financial office and with TerMolen. The plan was to organize a trip for a select number of trustees who, in Clements's judgment, would be most interested in the fort, so that they could see it firsthand. In July were two more meetings with TerMolen and his staff to plan the trip, now set for August 14.

Baker had secured the use of a plane owned and operated by Dresser Industries. A group of trustees consisting of Clements, C. A. Tatum (Chairman of the SMU Board of Trustees), Robert Ritchie, Eugene McDermott, and Floyd James (all trustees) were aboard, together with Baker and me. Wendorf was in residence at the fort, as was Terry, who was initiating his writers' workshop that year. My notes are not clear on this point, but I believe that TerMolen drove out and met us there. Wendorf had an appropriate schedule of events laid out, including a meeting with the Fort Burgwin Board and a visit to one of the ancient pueblo sites on the property. He had also arranged for a southwestern luncheon, complete with margaritas, in one of the compounds at the fort. After lunch, there was discussion about the potential of the property for the university and how best to achieve that potential. The conversation was enlivened but not necessarily enhanced by the quality of the luncheon libations!

In these early years, housing for faculty and students was a limitation. The restored fort provided offices, laboratories, a library, and classroom space. The officers' quarters consisted of a three-bedroom, a two-bedroom, and three efficiency apartments, which were used for faculty. The commanding officer's two-bedroom house was first occupied by Marian Meyers on a year-round basis, but by the early 1970s it became, and remains, the director's residence. Student housing was provided by a few buildings left over from the sawmill days. At best, these were primitive and of limited capacity. Better housing and dining facilities for students were clearly needed. During the spring and early summer of 1972, a number of conversations took place involving Wendorf, TerMolen and the development staff, Clements, and me. These meetings explored various concepts for the development of the fort and the programs that would be housed there.

At this time a strong graduate program was being developed in the SMU Department of History. One of the faculty additions to that program was Thomas Hughes, a scholar of the history of technology and engineering. He came to me in the spring of 1972 and asked if I knew of a quiet place where he could get away for the summer with his family to complete a book he'd been working on for several years. With some trepidation, I spoke with Wendorf, knowing how crowded Fort Burgwin was but also recognizing that an important function of the fort should be to provide exactly the kind of retreat Hughes was looking for. Fred very graciously juggled his already tight housing needs and made a place for Hughes to finish his book.

This illustrates the urgency of the housing situation. If the fort was to fulfill the potential that all of us, certainly including Clements, saw for it, we needed to begin to remedy the needs for student and, to some extent, faculty housing and for dining facilities. The Fort Burgwin Board met on August 5, 1972. Clements attended, as did I. At that time Clements and I also visited the John Young-Hunter estate on the eastern outskirts of Taos. Young-Hunter, a British portrait painter, had lived and worked in Taos before his death in 1955. Since the fort could not provide housing, the Young-Hunter home and grounds had been rented by the university from his estate in order to begin a program in painting and the visual arts in Taos. This proved the point not only that SMU needed to improve the housing situation at the fort but also that there was wide interest across the university in summer programs in appropriate subjects at Fort Burgwin.

On August 30, 1972, in Dallas, Clements, Robert Ritchie (SMU attorney and trustee), Bill Heroy Jr. (SMU Vice President for Finance), Wendorf, and I met to discuss next steps and strategies for housing development at Fort Burgwin. It was at this meeting that Clements outlined his concept for raising money to develop the fort. Through personal negotiations with the Rounds Foundation in Wichita, Kansas, Clements had secured essentially all of the remaining private acreage surrounding the fort for the university. With control of all of the surrounding private land, SMU was now in a position to begin to plan for the entire campus. Clements had conceived the idea of initiating substantial ground leases, on the nonacademic part of the campus, on which anyone making a $1 million gift or more to SMU would be invited to build an appropriate house. The donor would have use of the house as long as he or she and the spouse lived. When they both died, the property would revert to SMU and could then be "sold" to another million-dollar donor. Clements wanted a trip organized by the end of October to locate student housing and dining halls and also to locate housing sites for himself, Ritchie, and Heroy. We settled on the date of October 12 for the trip. We would fly in a new plane that SEDCO (Clements's company) had bought for its drilling activities in the Middle East—an Aero Commander that had a capacity of six plus the pilot. Making the trip were Clements, Ritchie, Wendorf, Heroy, Ed Hoffman (Director of the SMU Physical Plant), and me. We were to meet Louis Walker (from Santa Fe), Wendorf's architect of choice, at the fort.

We left the Addison, Texas, airport at 5:30 a.m. It was a beautiful, clear fall day, and the trip out was uneventful. We arrived at the Taos airport at about 9:00 a.m. and were met by Tito Archuleta, the caretaker at the fort. Wendorf had devoted a great deal of thought to what should be built and where. By the time we finished, ten dormitory casitas had been sited, along with a dining hall and a site for a large water tank to service the entire property. Additionally, Clements, Ritchie and Heroy had picked sites for their houses on the wooded bluff overlooking the Little Rio Grande and suitably far south of the casitas and dining hall that there would not be interference between the two areas. The dining hall and the residential casitas were to be Clements's first major gift to SMU in support of Fort Burgwin.

We returned to the airport and took off. After refueling in Santa Fe, we again took off. At 16,000 feet, just over the pass at the northern end of the Sandia Mountains southeast of Santa Fe, Hoffman looked out the window and said to the pilot, "Look at your starboard engine!" The engine was drenched in oil. The pilot immediately cut the engine and feathered the propeller. I think everyone assumed that we would return to Santa Fe, but the pilot said, "We are the same distance from Amarillo and Lubbock, and there's a lot better commercial service in Lubbock, so we are going there." It was quiet in the cabin, and Ritchie kept pointing out various landing fields we were passing over. Even though the port engine was under some strain, it maintained us at a gradually declining altitude until we landed in Lubbock. The control tower there kept asking the pilot to declare an emergency landing, but he refused on the grounds that it would require too much paperwork afterward. The only excitement of the landing was the fire engines lining the runway and the fact that the port brake shoe caught fire because it was having to offset the engine on that side. We completed the trip home to Dallas, on a commercial flight, without event.

Three days later, on October 15, Wendorf, Hoffman, and I flew to Albuquerque, met Walker in Santa Fe, and then drove to Taos, spending the sixteenth and the morning of the seventeenth staking foundations, positioning the water tank and lines, and completing as many tasks as possible so that construction could begin as early in the spring of 1973 as weather would permit. We left Fort Burgwin the afternoon of October 17 and returned to Dallas. My notes show a number of meetings related to Fort Burgwin scattered through the remainder of 1972 and the early months of 1973. These meetings were with TerMolen and others in the SMU Development Office, with Heroy and various people in the financial and physical plant area, and with William B. Stallcup (Professor of Biology and Associate Provost), Terry, and other leaders in the academic area. All these meetings concerned the development of the plant and programs at the fort. But perhaps the most important single event of that period was the reelection of Richard Nixon as President of the United States and the subsequent appointment of Clements as Deputy Secretary of Defense. This would, of course, have a significant impact both on Fort Burgwin and on the larger university.

Relations with the Board

By this time, members of the Fort Burgwin Board and I were getting to know each other well enough that they were beginning to contact me directly. This was difficult because the last thing any of us needed was for Wendorf not to be fully in charge. On the other hand, they needed to feel a growing comfort level with SMU, the institution to which they presumably would convey ownership of Fort Burgwin in 1979. In 1972 I was appointed Provost and Vice President for Academic Affairs of SMU. That position made my responsibilities for the nurture and development of Fort Burgwin even more critical. Therefore, it was important for Associate Provost Stallcup and me to keep ourselves involved in the Fort Burgwin program throughout the time that we were in those offices.

In the earlier chapters in this history, Wendorf has described his difficult relationship with Marian Meyers. That relationship was very much a factor in my relationship with the Board as well. Meyers was intensely loyal to the memory of Ralph Rounds. The fort reconstruction and related research center development had, after all, begun with Rounds and was wed—in her mind—to his memory. Thus it is unlikely that anyone with the responsibility of carrying the Fort Burgwin project forward could have avoided tensions with her, for I believe that she clung to the hope that Fort Burgwin could somehow continue as an independent entity, as she believed Rounds had envisioned it. My notes, phone logs, and travel schedules of the 1970s contain many records of calls and even special trips to Taos to deal with various Board concerns, many of which were traceable to Meyers's concerns. In these matters Jack Brandenburg, who by then was Board Chairman, and Paul Sears, the world-renowned botanist and environmentalist living in retirement in Taos and a member of the Fort Burgwin Board, were enormously helpful. Both were used to dealing with facts rather than speculation—and in every case, that was all that was required. I worked hard to maintain good relations with Meyers, and I believe I was successful. She also developed respect and affection for Terry, and this was very helpful. My goals throughout the decade of the 1970s were to make sure that we lived up to or exceeded the letter of SMU's agreement with the Fort Burgwin Board and, just as important, to bring the Board and the Taos community into a continuingly positive feeling toward the university. Many things and the actions of many people helped us accomplish those goals. Significant among these was the Colloquium Series begun by Wendorf and Ron Wetherington shortly after completion of the new dining hall, which provided a suitable venue for such events. Also helpful were the various musical events presented by the SMU Meadows School of the Arts faculty when they were in residence at the fort.

The acquisition of additional land, the construction of student casitas and the dining hall, the establishment of an enlarged educational program, and the development of cultural programs for the Taos community all signaled that SMU had more than lived up to its contractual commitments to the Fort Burgwin Board to develop the fort. The meeting of the Fort Burgwin Board on August 11, 1979, was harmonious, and the vote to convey the title for the

Burgwin property to SMU was unanimous. Under the terms of the agreement between the Fort Burgwin Board and SMU, the Fort Burgwin Board was to remain extant for another ten years—until 1989. This precaution was provided in the event that SMU should quit claim to ownership of the property, in which case title would revert to the Fort Burgwin Corporation. At the same meeting I, on behalf of SMU, also asked the Board members to continue on in an advisory capacity to the university with regard to the fort. A very important benchmark in the history of Fort Burgwin had been reached and passed!

Throughout my time of direct responsibility for Fort Burgwin and its programs (1969–84), the support, friendship, and many contributions of Brandenburg and Sears are treasured bright spots, as are the contributions of Ina MacNaughton. The completed conveyance of ownership to SMU in 1979 in a harmonious and positive fashion is due in no small part to their wise counsel and informed judgment. Others of course played important roles, but the steadiness, insightfulness, and leadership of these three mark them as truly special.

Research and Educational Programs

Research in archaeology has been carried on essentially continuously since the Fort Burgwin Research Center came into being. Research programs in geology and biology have been intermittent. With the completion in 1974 of the student casitas and the dining hall, more extensive programs for students became possible. The fort had been set up on the SMU books as a cost center (meaning that the expenses of operating the fort on a year-round basis needed to be covered by revenues earned in the summer—the only time the facility generated revenue—and that it received no support in the university's annual budget, other than the $10,000 committed in the original contract). So keeping the casitas in use as much as possible during the summer was important. With that in mind, SMU experimented with two types of programs. The university departed from a strict interpretation of the philosophy that courses taught at the fort should be of a nature to be enhanced by or appropriate to the environment there. It also departed from the guideline that only SMU-related courses would use the facilities. The geology field school in which the University of North Carolina was a participant provided a model for this program, and by the late 1970s, we were renting space to geology field schools from other universities, conspicuously the University of Texas. In those days we drew the line at pre-collegiate groups. There were frequent requests from youth groups—church-related and otherwise—but these did not fit the basic concept we had for the fort as a collegiate institution. More recently this barrier has been lowered, but in the early days it was strictly adhered to. In those early days SMU also offered a number of general-distribution courses required in the University College curriculum—courses such as "The Nature of Man" and "Discourse and Literature," courses that were not inappropriate for the fort but that were certainly not significantly improved by being taught there.

In the late 1970s Associate Provost Stallcup and I decided that we needed to begin to reverse some of these trends. Returning to the idea of a major focus on the three sciences of archaeology, biology, and geology, we found discretionary money in the SMU academic budget and said to each of the three departments: "We will add a position to your department faculty on the condition that the person you add will develop a full-time research and teaching program in that discipline at Fort Burgwin. We will view that person's full-time load to be the summer at Fort Burgwin, teaching and carrying on research on the Taos campus, and one of the two regular semesters carrying on teaching and research on the Dallas campus. The other semester in Dallas is free for research or vacation." Michael Dungan was appointed in geology, Anne Woosley in anthropology, and Donna Howell in biology. Dungan mounted a successful program in geology. He produced a series of recognized publications on the northern Rio Grande Rift, and a number of successful master's theses were also conducted in that area under his direction. In addition, Dungan organized and held at the fort two international research conferences. The quality of Dungan's work is attested to by the fact that he was invited to a named chair at the prestigious University of Geneva, Switzerland. Unfortunately, SMU was unable to make a suitable counter-offer. Woosley continued the active archaeological program at the fort and in the surrounding area. Among other activities carried on during her tenure was the organization at the fort of the Pecos Research Conference, the responsibility for which fell almost entirely on her. In the mid-1980s, she received an offer to become Resident Director of the Amerind Foundation, just outside Tucson, Arizona. This was a full-time, year-round appointment. She felt that she had accomplished much of what she had wanted to do at SMU and Fort Burgwin and thus elected to take the new position. Howell, meanwhile, joined a biology department that had relatively little emphasis on field biology, with most of the faculty being principally interested in molecular biology. Moreover, the relationship between Howell and her colleagues at Fort Burgwin was not a comfortable one, and so after a few years, she elected to leave. Overall, the impact of these appointments on the Fort Burgwin program in research and teaching was positive and significant. It is unfortunate that the appointments were not carried forward after the three initial appointees departed.

I believed then—and I still believe now—that this kind of support from the university administration is necessary to develop and maintain the program at the fort at its full potential. This program was sufficiently successful that it clearly warranted being continued by the university, but this has not happened. Current trends at the fort appear to belie the notion that much research goes on there other than the summer field schools in archaeology. That is unfortunate. It is this kind of research and serious teaching that, properly used, could set SMU apart as an institution of distinction!

The Physical Plant

An interesting facet of administering the fort in those early days was the fact that Stallcup and I were responsible for all aspects of the operation: academic program, student life, budget, and physical plant. These were interesting challenges and, as an old friend used to tell me, "learning experiences." The fort had, of course, a variety of architecture—from the vertical-log replicas of the original mid-nineteenth-century buildings to real-adobe and pseudo-adobe buildings of the casitas and dining hall, to small frame buildings left over from the sawmill days. Each type of architecture had its own needs and demands.

During my time with the fort, the head of the maintenance department was Tito Archuleta. His wife, Florida, ran the kitchen in the summer. During the winter they were in residence at the fort for basic maintenance and security. Each of them was responsible for hiring his or her own crew. All of their communications with their crews were in Spanish, and there were many times when it would have been a great help to me to be able to speak and understand Spanish. Even though there were things that I am sure could have been done better without the "cultural divide," by and large the Archuletas did a good job for the university, and we would have been hard-pressed to manage either the physical plant or the food service without them.

One of the perennial problems of the fort itself was its flat tar-and-gravel roofs, which leaked after every rain and all during the melt season in the spring. Anyone who has dealt with flat roofs knows the problem. Tito came to me in the late 1970s with a suggestion to solve the problem without upsetting the aesthetics of the fort. He proposed running a 2x12-inch ridge vertically down the long axis of each roof, then running tapered rafters perpendicularly from that ridge to the edge of the roof, and then putting neutral-colored roofing on the sheeting on top of those rafters. We agreed to experiment with one roof and to evaluate the aesthetic and mechanical effects. It was a great success. All roofs on the fort are now treated that way. They no longer leak, and the roof covering blends with the rustic surroundings of the fort. Tito gets the credit!

I was startled to arrive one spring in the late 1970s and discover that a portal had been added around the outer wall of the officers' quarters. Post Surgeon W. W. Anderson's 1850s drawings do not show a portal, and I knew that Wendorf had found no evidence of one when he had dug the foundations of the officers' quarters. But the portal did look good, and it was functional. I followed the old guideline, "When in doubt, do nothing!" Apparently, Tito had decided that a portal would improve the appearance and function of the building, and having the necessary materials in his storage shed, he had simply proceeded to build it, with no authorization from anyone. Predictably, and understandably, Wendorf was upset about the portal because of the departure from the faithful restoration of the original building. But I decided that the damage to be done in removing the portal could be a problem, so the portal is still there. Tito and Florida, for all the minor frustrations in dealing with them, were for many years the mainstays of the operation of Fort Burgwin. We would have been hard-pressed to function without them, and their presence year-round at the fort ensured a good relationship with the Hispanic community, of which they were highly regarded members.

Fort Burgwin at the Beach

At the Fort Burgwin Board meeting on August 15, 1976, a number of the Taos members were talking about the current civic conversation in Taos regarding the proposed dam to be built down the canyon (north) from Fort Burgwin—a dam that would impound a lake that would flood the Lavender Estates (a small upscale residential development immediately downstream—i.e., north—of the fort property) and encroach on the very northern end of the fort property, near the junction of the Little Rio Grande and Pot Creek. There was much talk but not much hard information. I did find out the name of the Albuquerque man who was in charge of the project. As soon as I returned to Dallas, I called and made an appointment to go to Albuquerque to visit with Warren Weber, of the U.S. Bureau of Reclamation.

During my visit, I found out that the plans were tentative and that the dam was being pushed by a local group who saw significant development opportunities for shoreline property. When I pointed out that much of the land was U.S. Forest Service land, Weber replied that there was enough private land that "the economics should work" if the developers could "work out easements with the Forest Service." I told him that at a minimum, there would have to be consideration for the significant impact that the dam would have on the Fort Burgwin property. When I inquired about New Mexico Highway 518 (which runs through the fort property), Weber said that the highway would be moved. I told him that we would insist on it being moved to a point outside the eastern boundary of the fort property (that move could actually have had a positive impact on the property). Finally, I told him that I would need to review this proposal both with the Fort Burgwin Board and with the university administration. When I returned to Dallas, I had telephone conversations with Brandenburg and with the SMU legal staff. I then called the office of U.S. Senator John Tower, a trustee of the university and a member of the Academic Affairs Committee of the Board (the committee with which I worked as Provost). I outlined the entire situation to him as I knew it, and he assigned a staff person to investigate the project and to let the Bureau and Forest Service know of the senator's personal interest in the matter.

Both in my dealings with Weber and in my dealings with the senator, I was careful to be evenhanded because I sensed that some of the Taos members of the Fort Burgwin Board had positive feelings about the lake. On the other hand, my clear responsibility was to the fort and to the university. As it turned out, I heard nothing more about the dam or the lake from anyone; nor did the senator's office. We eventually concluded that the matter had died. On a personal level, I was relieved, because the project would have significantly altered the environs of the fort. Moreover, it would have totally inundated St. Vrain's Mill, a historically important site farther down the canyon. Sometime later a couple of the Board members, in a half-joking way, chided me about "killing the lake project," so my evenhandedness may have been for naught.

New Buildings

By the late 1970s, I had been in discussions with Clements and the university about additional buildings that were needed at Fort Burgwin. It was clear to me then that we would need expertise well beyond mine not only in terms of building new buildings but also in terms of better maintaining the existing buildings. We knew that using the SMU Physical Plant Department would be relatively expensive and that doing so would put a strain on the fort's budget. Nonetheless, with things progressing smoothly toward the passing of the title for the fort property to the university in 1979, it was only a matter of time until Fort Burgwin was fully integrated into SMU. Thus we moved to get Dick Arnett and H. R. Patterson, of the SMU Physical Plant Department, fully involved with the Fort Burgwin Campus.

One of the urgent needs to support the research program in archaeology was a facility for the preparation and cataloging of artifacts and a secure facility for their storage. The original hospital and the surgeon's quarters had been in a combined building on the south side of the parade ground of the original fort compound. The foundations of the building had been dug in the initial phase of defining the layout of the fort. Now, with the thought that this building was the appropriate size for an artifact curation center, I asked Woosley during the 1981 field season to redig the foundation, marking the boundaries very carefully so that the architect could locate the restored building on the exact footprint of the original. With Tito's portal on the adjacent officers' quarters clearly in mind, I asked Woosley to be especially alert to determine whether there had been a portal on the front (north) side of the original hospital. After the foundations had been completely dug and marked out, Woosley assured me that she had found a "drip line" marking the front edge of a portal on the north side of the hospital, and so I instructed the architect (Walker) to draw the plans with a portal. (After this decision was made, I learned that other archaeologists question Woosley's identification of a "drip line.") Walker made drawings and sketches for the curation facility during the winter of 1981–82. On August 20, 1982, I met with Clements at his house adjacent to the fort and proposed that we restore the hospital and surgeon's quarters as a curation facility following Walker's drawings. Clements agreed to fund the project, and that evening he, Mrs. Clements, Woosley, and I had dinner at the La Dona Luz Restaurant in Taos to celebrate.

The construction of the facility began in the spring of 1983, under the supervision of Arnett and Patterson from SMU. The contract was let to Mr. Maestas, coincidentally a nephew of Florida Archuleta's. This initially appeared to be an ideal arrangement. However, one night, as construction was starting in the early spring, Arnett received a call from a very distraught Florida, who informed him that Tito and her nephew were literally in a stand-off with drawn guns and that she was standing between them to keep them from shooting each other. The next day Arnett and Patterson flew from Dallas to Taos to sort out the problem. They were successful in developing guidelines and clearly defined lines of authority that enabled the project to go forward, but it was at best an uneasy truce.

In 1983, during one of my regular briefings with Clements, he asked me about long-range plans and long-range needs. At that time I laid out for him a proposal for additional faculty housing and for a permanent residence for the caretaker. We discussed the fact that the officers' quarters at the fort had barely been adequate for the faculty when the number of students coming to fort was smaller. Now, with the new casitas and with some faculty involved in research, we were seriously limited by the amount of faculty housing. I recommended building three faculty duplexes, each housing two faculty couples. Clements then authorized me to have Walker prepare the plans for our review.

I also mentioned to Clements that it had been an imposition on the Archuletas to have to move back and forth every year between their own home in Talpa and the fort. (As the demand for housing had increased, the Archuletas had been asked to move back to their own house in Talpa during the summer.) I suggested that we build a year-round caretaker's residence—a comfortable two- or three-bedroom adobe house. I further suggested that we site the residence where it would be separate from the fort and, very important, where it would be close to the main gate so that it could have a monitoring effect when the fort had a low population of faculty and students and thus was more vulnerable. I also pointed out that when the Archuletas retired, such a building would likely be a recruiting inducement to their successors. Clements thought that this was a very good idea, and we agreed that Walker should prepare drawings for that project as well.

One of my last official acts as the administrator responsible for the fort, in the autumn of 1984 when my wife and I were at the fort on leave, was to meet with Clements and Bill Hutchison, both SMU Trustees, with Walker, and with James Judge, the director-designate of the fort, to agree on the locations of the faculty houses and the caretaker's house. Walker had originally proposed to locate the faculty houses on the floodplain immediately adjacent to the Little Rio Grande. My strong recommendation was to position them on the higher surface above the current floodplain, and they were staked in that position. I learned somewhat later that the architect had placed the septic tanks for the three units topographically above the houses, so that a sump pump is now required.

Staffing

As Wendorf has noted, Ronald Wetherington was appointed to succeed him as Director of Fort Burgwin in April 1976. Wetherington left that post in 1977, and Thomas E. Williams, Professor of Geology, was appointed to succeed him. At that time the director still had full responsibility for all phases of the operation, including the physical plant and student life. Williams handled all of this effectively, including patrolling the residential area at night to make sure that everything was in order. The growing program and the administrative demands of the directorship meant that by then, the director had little—if any—time for his own scientific pursuits. In the summer of 1980 I left the provost's office to become President ad Interim of SMU and ultimately President of the Institute for the Study of Earth and Man (ISEM) at SMU. Part of my exit agreement with the university provided that I would keep the administrative responsibility for Fort Burgwin when I went to the Institute. At this time Williams expressed a strong desire to be relieved of the Fort Burgwin responsibility, and we agreed.

As I phased out of university administration, I had a bit more flexibility in my schedule but not enough to enable me to be in residence full-time at the fort. I thought about William Pearce, who had been a Fort Burgwin Board member and had had a long and distinguished career on the history faculty at Texas Tech. He had recently retired as President of Texas Wesleyan University in Fort Worth. He and his wife knew and loved Taos and Fort Burgwin, and so in 1981 SMU invited Pearce to spend a couple of summers as Resident Director at the fort. I was able to provide more support than in the past, which was important because the fort was then in a growth phase and needed someone in Taos as well as a continuing presence in Dallas. For health reasons, Pearce was unable to continue into the summer of 1983. Charles Dodge, formerly Professor of Geology at the University of Texas at Arlington and then Adjunct Professor of Geology at SMU, agreed to serve as Resident Director for one summer. Finally, in the summer of 1984, Stallcup who by then had left the SMU Provost's Office, agreed to serve as Resident Director.

Another facet of staffing at Fort Burgwin relates to student life. By 1980 it was clear that in addition to assistance in the physical plant area, the director also needed assistance in the area of student life. The casitas were now running at or near capacity. The courses being offered were diverse, and the student body was likewise diverse. When all the Fort Burgwin students had been focused in two or three field courses requiring a good deal of work in the evenings—completing maps, writing notes, and so forth—discipline was a relatively small problem. But with the diversity of courses came fewer evening assignments and more time for other activities. In addition to the interpersonal relationships among the students, there was the matter of preventing damage to the university's property. With these things in mind, I approached Walter Snickenberger, SMU Vice President for Student Affairs, and asked him to consider assigning one of his experienced staff to the fort for the two summer months. He was most agreeable and assigned Associate Dean Bill McIntyre, who served effectively in the role for a number of summers.

By the early 1980s, the Fort Burgwin property had been officially conveyed to SMU. More programs were being developed at the fort, although the research programs (except for the one in archaeology) were still flagging. It was clearly time to fully integrate the fort into the mainline operations of the university. It was also time, I thought, to appoint a full-time director (as opposed to a faculty member who did this during the summer) to accomplish this task. In spite of my agreement that the fort would stay administratively under the ISEM, I felt that it should return to the Provost's Office. I recommended these actions to the new provost, Hans Hillerbrand, and he and I agreed that I would conclude my responsibilities for Fort Burgwin at the end of December 1984.

The Search for a New Director

In the spring of 1984 Provost Hillerbrand asked me to chair an advisory search committee to find a full-time director for Fort Burgwin. Also on the committee were Tom Williams and a Department of Anthropology representative (whose name is not in my notes). With the considerable help of Fred Wendorf, a designated consultant to the committee, we assembled a list of qualified candidates. They were interviewed in the early summer of 1984. Our final recommendation to the provost was James Judge. Judge met informally with the members of the Fort Burgwin Board at their August 1984 meeting. Hillerbrand then accepted the recommendation of the search committee and appointed Judge as the new director of Fort Burgwin, effective January 1, 1985.

I was on leave in the fall of 1984 and was in residence at the fort during part of this time. Judge made at least two visits to the fort for consultation and planning. With a mixture of feelings, I turned the responsibilities for Fort Burgwin over to him at the end of the fall semester of 1984. I knew that we had accomplished Wendorf's and Albritton's goal of establishing Fort Burgwin as a part of SMU and that the physical plant at the fort had progressed dramatically and was continuing to grow. I also knew that the fort was playing a growing role in the intellectual life of SMU. But I was concerned that its potential as a significant research center was not (and, I think, still is not) moving toward realization. And of course, there were still many things to accomplish, which is often the case at times of transition. Nonetheless, all of us who were associated with the fort during these years can take real pride and pleasure in what was accomplished at Fort Burgwin during its transition into SMU-in-Taos.

I have continued my association with Fort Burgwin since 1984 as a member of the Advisory Board—a total relationship of thirty-eight years. I am very grateful for the progress we have been able to make there. The continuing and very generous support (both financial and personal) of Governor Clements and his friends has made an enormous difference! In fact, SMU might very well not have been able to mount a successful program at the fort without this support. The combination of Clements's interest and support and his presence there has been of basic importance to Wendorf, to me, and to those who have followed us in building Fort Burgwin and its programs. All of us are deeply grateful for Bill's interest, support, and friendship. Also essential in almost every phase of my adminstrative activities at the fort was the advice and tireless participation of Associate Provost Bill Stallcup, for which I will always be deeply grateful.

It is gratifying to me that the university has now included Fort Burgwin in the planning for its coming capital campaign. When this is successfully completed, SMU-in-Taos, as Fort Burgwin is now called, will be able to take another major step forward. Although the program there has not developed in the way in which we had originally envisioned it, Fort Burgwin, in its beautiful valley, has clearly caught the interest of the university administration and of a supportive group of trustees and friends. The prospects are bright, and our efforts of the past are indeed bearing fruit and being validated!

Figure 29.

William Clements, SMU President Gerald Turner, and Fred Wendorf at the dedication of the Wendorf Information Commons at Fort Burgwin, July 2004.

Photo by Hillsman Jackson. Photo courtesy of Southern Methodist University photo archives.

Epilogue

From the time I left in 1976 until today, Fort Burgwin has had six directors and acting directors. For much of this time, Fort Burgwin has continued its struggle to establish a role in the academic life of SMU. Fort Burgwin, however, has not stood still. The campus has undergone a number of important improvements, including the addition of a new archaeology laboratory and collection facility where the old hospital had been, as well as three duplex faculty houses with a total of six two-bedroom apartments, a laundry building, and two tennis courts, all built with funds contributed by Bill and Rita Clements. In addition, a dance/music/auditorium building was built with funds given by Peter and Edith O'Donnell.

As this memoir was being completed in the fall of 2006, and again through the generosity of the Clements and two anonymous donors, a library/computer building was built on the footprint of a cantonment warehouse located next to the archaeology laboratory. This new library/computer facility is a major addition to the fort's academic facilities. It is of particular interest to me because Bill and Rita Clements and the two anonymous donors asked that this new building be named the "Fred Wendorf Information Commons." Several hundred participants so honored me at a special meeting at Fort Burgwin in July 2004 (Figure 29). This signal honor came as a complete surprise to me and my wife, Christy Bednar (Figure 30).

My North American library will be housed in this new information commons, which has twenty-five high-speed computers, as well as scanners and high-speed printers, for faculty and student use. I share the gratitude of everyone at SMU for the generosity of Bill and Rita Clements and the two anonymous

Figure 30.

Fred Wendorf and Christy Bednar with the dedication plaque, July 2004.

Photographer unknown. Photo courtesy of Fred Wendorf.

donors in providing this splendid addition to the resources at Fort Burgwin and to SMU. They have made Fort Burgwin a delightful place for SMU students to study and learn about the beauty of nature and the diversity of our world.

The Fort Burgwin campus remains a beautiful and restful setting for a wide variety of academic programs. It is, however, no longer known as the "Fort Burgwin Research Center." The "Research Center" part of the name was removed from the gate in 1995 to emphasize that this is no longer a research facility but, rather, an educational and training institution. It is now known as "Southern Methodist University in Taos at Fort Burgwin," or simply as "SMU-in-Taos." Whatever the name, I am sure that Ralph Rounds would be pleased to see what has become of his idea. His vision has been altered a bit, but in many ways I think he would feel that the result is better. I know I do. Had Ralph Rounds lived, we might have filled this valley with homes, put in ski lifts and other economic developments, and made it more like Aspen. Doing so would have changed this quiet valley forever—not, I think, for the better. Today, the Carson National Forest surrounds the Fort Burgwin campus on three sides. Summers find the Fort Burgwin campus filled with bright young people studying all sorts of subjects, from archaeology to zoology. At least one evening a week, sometimes more often, from one hundred to two hundred people from the Taos area come to the campus, enjoying lectures by distinguished scholars from all over the country, listening to recitals by prominent musicians, or seeing exhibits or watching plays given by students from the SMU Meadows School of the Arts. In these and many other ways, SMU and its friends, faculty, and students have not only benefited from the vision and generosity of Ralph Rounds; they have also succeeded in fulfilling his goal of "enriching the intellectual and cultural life of this part of New Mexico."

About the Authors

Christy Bednar

AFTER SERVING IN THE U.S. ARMY DURING WORLD WAR II, FRED WENDORF earned a B.A. in Anthropology from the University of Arizona and a Ph.D. from Harvard University. He served as a curator and later as Director of Research and Associate Director of the Museum of New Mexico before becoming Director of the Fort Burgwin Research Center in Taos, N.M., in 1956, a position he held for 20 years. In 1964 he joined the faculty at Southern Methodist University, where he was the founding chairman of the nationally recognized Department of Anthropology. He retired from SMU in 2002, but he retains an office there, where he continues his research and writing.

Wendorf's work as an archaeologist has led to many awards and honors, including election to the National Academy of Sciences (1987) and receiving the prestigious Lucy Wharton Drexel Medal for Archaeological Achievement in 1996 (awarded every five years). He has served as President of the Society for American Archaeology and the Society of Professional Archaeologists. He has written or assembled and edited more than 30 books and 150 articles.

JAMES E. BROOKS received a Ph.D. in Geology from the University of Washington (Seattle), an M.S. in Geology from Northwestern University, and an A.B. in Geology from DePauw University. In 1952 he joined the faculty of Southern Methodist University, where he served at various times as Chair of the Geological Sciences Department, Dean of the College of Humanities and Sciences, Associate Provost, Provost, and President Ad Interim. A former President of the Institute for the Study of Earth and Man (ISEM) at SMU, he is currently Chairman of the ISEM Foundation. Brooks is a Fellow of the American Association for the Advancement of Science, the Geological Society of America, the Texas Academy of Science, and the Explorer's Club, and is a member of the American Association of Petroleum Geologists.